THE *unstoppable* SHERO♀

DR. BARBARA WALKER-GREEN

THE *unstoppable* SHERO

A WOMAN'S GUIDE TO **THRIVING** IN A **RESISTANT** WORLD

Advantage | Books

Published by Advantage Books, Charleston, South Carolina.
An imprint of Advantage Media.

ADVANTAGE is a registered trademark, and the Advantage colophon is a trademark of Advantage Media Group, Inc.

Printed in the United States of America.

10 9 8 7 6 5 4 3 2 1

ISBN: 979-8-89188-151-8 (Hardcover)
ISBN: 979-8-89188-152-5 (eBook)

Library of Congress Control Number: 2024926448

Cover design by Analisa Smith.
Layout design by Matthew Morse.

This publication is designed to provide accurate and authoritative information in regard to the subject matter covered. It is sold with the understanding that the publisher is not engaged in rendering legal, accounting, or other professional services. If legal advice or other expert assistance is required, the services of a competent professional person should be sought.

Advantage Books is an imprint of Advantage Media Group. Advantage Media helps busy entrepreneurs, CEOs, and leaders write and publish a book to grow their business and become the authority in their field. Advantage authors comprise an exclusive community of industry professionals, idea-makers, and thought leaders. For more information go to **advantagemedia.com**.

To my mother, Maxine Green—

Your quiet strength, gentle resilience, and unwavering love have been my greatest inspiration. This is for you, always.”

Contents

Foreword

The Unstoppable Shero: A Woman's Guide to Thriving in a Resistant World is dedicated to women of all ages. Women, this book is a call to action and your road map to succeed in life. I wish I'd had this book when I entered the male-dominated workforce in my twenties.

In *The Unstoppable Shero*, Dr. Barbara Walker-Green examines the challenges and triumphs of the journey that successful women have endured to become sheroes and agents of change. She shares internal struggles, self-doubt, and fears that have held women back for centuries, pointing out the obstacles that threaten to undermine the progress of the shero within. These fears can slow you down and prevent you from obtaining your goals.

Let this book serve as a wake-up call to all women: you have a responsibility to yourself and to others. Light that fire within you, rise up and confront the barriers, and never give up on yourself and others. As you climb the ladder of success, reach back and pull someone up.

You must equip yourself through thought, study, and experience. Stay vigilant, and stay alert. As 2 Timothy 1:7 says, "For God has not given us a spirit of fear and timidity, but of power, love, and self-discipline."

Smiles and love,

Judge Maria T. Jackson

339th State District Court in Houston, Harris County, Texas

Acknowledgments

I am filled with deep gratitude and a profound sense of appreciation for those who have had a significant impact on my life, often in ways they may not even realize. First and foremost, I want to acknowledge my remarkable mother, my ultimate shero. As a mother of seven, she has showered us with unconditional love and shown us the true meaning of family, teaching us to support and care for one another even in the face of adversity.

Additionally, I want to recognize my incredible children, Shaolin and Julian Walker, who hold a special place in my heart and form the core of my inner circle. They are my "why" in life, and together, we have embraced a family mantra that we call "three-deep." This mantra represents our commitment to passing down pillars of wealth for at least three generations. We understand that true wealth extends beyond monetary assets and encompasses the rich tapestry of traditions, self-reflection, and knowledge of how to strive for personal excellence.

Passing on the legacy of knowing one's history and defining one's purpose in life is a responsibility that we actively and intentionally undertake. My children are fully aware of their role in upholding the principles of three-deep and are dedicated to preserving and expanding this legacy. With the arrival of my first grandson, Jayceland Skies Castleberry, now two years old, and my second grandson, Miles

Jaylen Walker, the stakes feel even higher. They represent the second generation, and the thought of what we can achieve for them fills me with fearless determination. Rather than allowing fear to hold me back, I channel it as fuel to propel myself toward my goals.

I actively engage in the process of passing down these pillars of wealth to my children, my beloved grandsons, and the generations to come. It is my fervent prayer that I have the privilege of witnessing the fruits of this legacy as they transcend multiple generations. I aspire to live a life that leaves an enduring impact and instills a sense of purpose, prosperity, and unity in my family for years to come. As a bonus, I now have a wonderful daughter-in-law, Nadja Walker, who is a blessing to our family. She brings joy, love, and an adventurous spirit to our family and loves and uplifts my son. I couldn't ask for better!

I acknowledge my sisters and brothers: Rosetta, Carolyn, Robert, Sharon, Johnnie, and Kenny. Without them in my life, I would not be who I am. Each and every one of them touches me in a different way, just as I do them. We are strong; we are united, and that is what has made us all so special to each other. We see each other as sisters and brothers; that is it. Though our brother, Johnnie, is not here with us physically, he is alive and well in our spirits. As our brother Robert lies resting in a convalescent hospital, our love for him remains as strong as ever. I acknowledge you all. I love you all.

I give special acknowledgment to my doctoral chairperson, Dr. Kriesta Watson. Dr. Kri, I listened to you! I hope to make you proud. Without your words of conviction, I would not be on this journey today. Rest in peace, dear friend.

I am deeply grateful to my new friend, Dr. Marilyn Kern-Foxworth, whose invaluable guidance and insights have added so much depth and meaning to *The Unstoppable Shero*. A trailblazer in her own right, Marilyn's expertise and inspiration have been a true gift on this journey, and I am honored to have her support.

Finally, I acknowledge those in my life who mean so much to me—my friends, my colleagues, my clients, those who work alongside me, and those who encourage me. There are so many of you out there. You all know who you are, and I love each of you.

Introduction

The day I told my high school guidance counselor that I wanted to be a lawyer, she laughed in my face. Not just a chuckle, but a full, dismissive laugh that echoed through the room. For years, that laugh haunted me—it echoed in my mind, nearly crushing my young spirit. It could have shattered my dreams, but instead it became the fuel that drove me. That laugh, meant to diminish me, only made me more determined to prove her wrong.

Just as that laugh once haunted me, many of us face the silent yet powerful forces of society's expectations, trying to navigate a world where social norms are often designed to confine us. The doubts and dismissals we encounter can weigh us down, making us question our worth and potential. But it's in confronting these challenges that we find our true strength, the strength to break free and redefine our own path.

The journey of writing this book has been a profound reflection of my life's path—a path that stretches from the memories of my past, through the challenges I've faced, to the clarity of my future. These pages are more than just a recounting of experiences; they are an intimate sharing of the lessons I've learned, the strength I've discovered, and the growth I've embraced. My hope is that, as you read, you will find in these stories not only a reflection of your own life but also a guide to recognizing the often silent forces shaping your decisions. It is an invitation to awaken the shero within you and to take command of your life's narrative.

My journey has been a powerful testament to the strength and resilience needed to navigate and overcome societal barriers. From the early days, when I faced doubt and discouragement, to where I stand now as a trailblazing entrepreneur and a leader in the financial industry, I've never wavered in my commitment to empowering others. My accomplishments across various industries, from building my own financial firm to becoming a trusted advisor to families, entrepreneurs, and businesses across the country, reflect my dedication to continually strive for growth and impact. I've worked with hundreds of clients over my twenty-year career, helping them secure their financial futures through innovative investment strategies and wealth management solutions. As an advocate for women's empowerment, I've authored two influential books and launched a podcast that gives women a platform to share their stories and strategies for success. Through my leadership and vision, I've not only broken barriers for myself but have also created opportunities for others to rise, empowering a new generation of entrepreneurs, advocates, and thought leaders. I've created opportunities not just for myself but for countless others, proving that true success lies in helping others achieve their potential. In this book, I invite you to break free from the limitations imposed by society and discover the power within yourself to rewrite your own narrative.

Through the challenges of corporate life, the trials of motherhood, and the transition into entrepreneurship, I began to see clearly the forces that had shaped my decisions. Mindsets and societal norms that sought to bind and define me were revealed for what they were—barriers to my true potential.

This book serves as a critical examination of how Social Role and Role Congruity Theories shape mindsets that can confine women, stifling their growth and potential. These mindsets often perpetuate stereotypes that limit women's opportunities. Other concepts like the Glass Ceiling and the Glass Cliff illustrate the dual challenge faced by women; while the Glass Ceiling represents the invisible barriers that prevent them from ascending to higher roles, the Glass Cliff signifies the precarious nature of the positions they do attain, often placing them in riskier situations. By understanding and addressing these societal constraints, we can develop strategies to dismantle them and foster an environment where women can thrive authentically and confidently.

This book is not just a chronicle of my life's challenges and triumphs; it is a call to action. It is a reminder that the binding mindsets of society are only as strong as we allow them to be. The true power lies in our realization of their fragility and our decision to rise above them. The journey of the shero is one of awakening, of reclaiming our power as women, and of using that power to reshape our world. It is a journey from a place of fight, hurt, and manipulation to a place of strength, love, and self-determination.

As you read, I encourage you to reflect on your own life. Recognize the silent realities that may be influencing your decisions and consider how you can take control of your life's narrative. Awaken the shero within, embrace your unique strengths, and redefine what it means to be a woman in today's world. This is not just my story—it is the story of all women who have faced challenges, broken through barriers, and emerged stronger on the other side. Points of reflection are strategically placed so that you can reflect in real time on the content and constructs and think about your own experiences and what the alternatives may be. Together, we can continue this journey of awakening and evolution, transforming our lives and the world around us.

As we embark on chapter one, we will examine the mindsets that bind us, focusing particularly on Social Role Theory and Role

Congruity Theory. Understanding these frameworks is crucial, as they shed light on how societal expectations can shape our identities and influence our interactions with others. By investigating these concepts, we aim to unravel the ways in which they impact our self-perception and relationships, ultimately empowering you to break free from limiting beliefs and embrace a more authentic self.

CHAPTER 1

Mindsets That Bind

I am not free while any woman is unfree,
even when her shackles are very different from my own.
—AUDRE LORDE

As a young girl, I remember growing up in a state of quiet desperation. Watching the world around me evolve and people navigate through it, I seemed to have little control over where my life would go. At the time, the societal expectations for a young African American female were bleak at best. Nothing that society revealed to me allowed me to believe that my life could be remarkable. I was merely a child when my father passed away. Losing my dad devastated our family and thrust my mother into the role of sole provider. As a young girl witnessing these trials, I unknowingly stepped into a world where societal norms, expectations, and prejudices would shape my path. In this chapter, I will unravel the complex interplay of theories that have emerged over time, explaining how they help us understand the socially ingrained behaviors that profoundly impacted my journey and continue to shape the narratives of women's lives worldwide.

We begin this journey with an in-depth look into the societal and cultural constructs that have formed the challenges we face as women. Theories such as Social Role Theory, Role Congruity Theory, and Glass

Cliff Theory have emerged from these constructs. They will help us understand the foundation of the challenges we continually encounter.

Understanding these theoretical frameworks is not just a matter of academic interest; it is essential for realizing the complexity and depth of our obstacles. This understanding equips us with the knowledge to confront these challenges with resilience, grit, and determination. We'll unravel the patterns perpetuating these obstacles through historical accounts and research. But beyond the theories and research, we will explore the personal experiences and stories of women who have navigated these challenging paths and emerged victorious. Their stories are a testament to their strength and perseverance, paving the way for future generations of women leaders and contributing to the rise of a strong Shero Nation. As a fellow woman and leader, you will find that these stories offer relevant and insightful glimpses into the social conditions that limit women even today and how the trailblazers before us tackled these challenges. More importantly, they guide us, current and future generations of women, to understand what we're up against and how we can navigate and ultimately overcome these obstacles. So let's embark on this transformative journey together, traversing the landscapes of shifting mindsets, challenging circumstances, and personal growth. Let's explore the crux of the obstacles that seek to limit our potential and advancement, starting with the theories that explain the social and cultural teachings that bind us.

A BLAST FROM THE PAST

Being hindered is nothing new for women. Women like us have been subjected to societal limitations and skepticism about our talents and true worth for centuries. Since the days of our founding fathers, women have fought to be recognized as equals in the citizenry of the

United States. John Adams's wife made her thoughts known about the issue. In the awakening and birth of a new nation, Abigail Adams wrote a passionate letter to her husband and other members of the Continental Congress:

> I long to hear that you have declared an independence—and by the way, in the new code of laws which I suppose it will be necessary for you to make, I desire you to remember the ladies and be more generous and favorable to them than your ancestors. Do not put such unlimited power into the hands of the husbands. Remember, all men would be tyrants if they could. If particular care and attention is not paid to the ladies, we are determined to foment a rebellion, and will not hold ourselves bound by any laws in which we have no voice or representation.[1]

Nearly 150 years before the ratification of the 19th Amendment, Abigail Adams fearlessly penned words that challenged the status quo. She told leading men that a change must occur. Otherwise, women would not sit quietly and go along with the way things were. She was a boss in her own right because she said what others would not. Her eloquence urged her husband and his peers to consider women's rights. The men paid attention. For instance, John Adams responded to Abigail's letters, showing that her words had a significant impact. Although this occurrence did not achieve full equality immediately, the attention her letters received from influential men of the time marked an early step toward recognizing and addressing women's issues. Yet it took a century after Adams's time before women secured the right to vote. Her powerful sentiments encountered considerable resistance. Even today, her impassioned stance would face a certain level of opposition. Within this resistance lies a complex tapestry of mindsets shaped by cultural systems and societal norms that continue to permeate our world. In writing this book, I took some time to think about our fight in the past and what it entailed. Reflecting on history helped me identify the conglomerate of traditions and attitudes that shape widely accepted theories, norms, and systems. I deepen my reflection in this chapter by examining the theories explaining harmful mindsets limiting women and society.

This chapter speaks to ingrained ideals that grip the very movement of women in society today. As women, social expectations have affected and somewhat controlled us for thousands of years. Most social constructs in Western culture directly affect how we pattern and move through our journeys; examining ingrained prejudices and social conditions through developed theories related to social expectations helps us understand the factors that hold women back. By analyzing these theories, we can clear a path to push aside old belief systems, paving the way for a smoother journey toward equality and empowerment.

NORMS AND LIMITATIONS—SOCIAL THEORIES OF MINDSETS THAT BIND

The journey we are about to take through the pages of this book will include a whirlwind of unfamiliar concepts. These concepts will set the stage for understanding the challenges that women have faced and continue to face from a new perspective. We will take a walk along the path that women before us walked while shining a bright light on the hidden forces directly affecting the movement of women in society.

Note the underlying conflict: hidden forces acting against women's forward movement versus sheroes making progressive steps despite those hidden forces. The shero concept speaks to the "she-hero" that women evolve into as we fight for our basic human rights. For now, we will delve into the hidden shackles that have bound women throughout history.

Clearly, we as women possess the potential and skill set to effectively lead in a variety of ways. However, the numerous barriers that limit our opportunities to do so are not as evident. Role Congruity Theory, Social Role Theory, and Glass Cliff Theory describe the deeply ingrained mindsets and widespread biases that hinder our progress into the upper echelons of leadership in America and around the world. In this chapter, I discuss each theory and explain the norms and structures that contribute to these obstacles.

CAREER STEREOTYPE PARADOX—
ROLE CONGRUITY THEORY

A girl should be two things: who and what she wants.
—COCO CHANEL

Role Congruity Theory explains the grossly unequal number of women in top-level management.[2] This theory is based on a perceived incongruity between the attributes of strong leaders and attributes assigned by social norms to women's gender roles. Incongruity simply means that saying a woman can be a strong leader is a contradiction. This theory proposes a perceived incongruity between male and female leadership ability, leading to gender-biased prejudices.[3] These prejudices include the perception that women are less effective than men in leadership roles.

Society often ponders comparison questions such as, "Who makes more competent leaders, men or women? Are men better than women at leading? Can women step up to the [leadership] plate?" Do not be fooled. These are not innocent questions. They are not posed out of curiosity. Unfortunately, questions like these have a nuance—a bias against us women.

Role Congruity Theory explains the root cause behind this type of inquiry. It also uncovers inconspicuous tones of partiality for our male counterparts. This theory examines widely accepted gender roles to compare our leadership to that of men. It begins to explain the "why" behind a doubting mindset regarding our abilities to lead. It also sheds light on the lagging representation of women in leadership roles. This theory emerged from the broader concept of gender roles, which are societal norms dictating the behaviors considered appropriate for men and women. Researchers noticed a pattern where women in leadership roles, or those aspiring to such roles, faced greater resistance compared to their male counterparts. This resistance was attributed to the discrepancy between the public's prescribed roles for women—nurturing, submissive, and communal—and the characteristics commonly associated with leadership—assertive, dominant, and agentic.

In examining this theory, scholars reviewed a wide array of evidence, including psychological experiments, meta-analyses, and real-world case studies. They found that both men and women tend to perceive female leaders less favorably, even when their performance was on par with male leaders. Studies highlighted that this bias led to harsher evaluations and more significant professional obstacles for women, with female leaders often being judged as either too soft or too harsh, irrespective of their actual leadership style. This body of evidence conclusively pointed to the lasting impact of societal stereotypes, revealing the structural barriers that contribute to gender inequality in leadership roles.

Simply put, Role Congruity Theory implies that women and power do not go together. This mindset is so deeply ingrained in the collective mindset of society, many individuals are resistant to immediate change.

It is crucial for us to carefully examine and dismantle these theories together, as we strive to demolish their power and create more equitable social expectations.

A PERSONAL NOTE

Part of my evolution that preceded my awakening included experiencing the effects of Role Congruity Theory. For a while, it silently dictated what I sought to become. Right at the beginning of my career, I began to understand that it was almost inconceivable that a woman, especially a Black woman, sought to become a doctor or a lawyer. In fact, it was seen as incongruent—or simply put, mutually exclusive ideals—for a female to become a doctor. In my corporate life, I was always considered for positions "suitable for a woman." Since it was the expectation at that time, I did not think any differently. I can now see how that accepted norm held me back from pursuing more male-dominated industries and positions early in my career.

REAL-LIFE ROLE CONGRUITY

One real-life example of Role Congruity Theory at work can be seen in the case of Marissa Mayer's tenure as CEO of Yahoo.

Marissa Mayer, a highly accomplished executive with a background in technology and a successful career at Google, was appointed as the CEO of Yahoo in 2012. Her appointment was initially met with significant attention and optimism, as she was tasked with revitalizing a struggling internet giant.

However, throughout her tenure, Mayer faced intense scrutiny and criticism, much of which can be attributed to gender biases influenced by social beliefs explained by Role Congruity Theory. Despite her proven track record and qualifications, Mayer was often subjected to gendered criticisms and stereotypes.

For example, Mayer's leadership style and decisions were frequently scrutinized in a manner that seemed to focus more on her gender than on her performance. Her approach to work, such as her decision to end telecommuting at Yahoo, was often criticized in ways that seemed to reflect gendered expectations of leadership behavior.

Additionally, Mayer's pregnancy and subsequent maternity leave became subjects of public debate, with some questioning her ability to effectively lead the company while also being a mother. These criticisms reflected entrenched stereotypes about women's roles in the workplace and society, suggesting that women cannot successfully balance career and family responsibilities.

Despite facing these challenges, Mayer made efforts to turn around Yahoo's fortunes, implementing various initiatives and acquisitions aimed at revitalizing the company. However, her tenure ultimately ended without achieving the desired turnaround for Yahoo.

Mayer's experience highlights how Role Congruity Theory explains perceptions of women in leadership positions, which often lead to biased criticisms and expectations that are not applied to male counterparts in similar roles. Her story underscores the importance of understanding binding theories so that our inevitable evolution to overcome them can be met with our eyes wide open.

POINT OF REFLECTION

Consider the following question to reflect on how Role Congruity Theory may manifest in your own life and experiences:

Have you ever found yourself making assumptions or judgments about someone's leadership abilities based on their gender? Reflect on instances where you may have unintentionally perpetuated stereotypes about who is "fit" for leadership roles. How might these biases impact your interactions and decisions in professional or personal settings?

IDENTITY EXPECTATIONS— SOCIAL ROLE THEORY

Social Role Theory is based on the principle that men and women behave differently in social situations and should take on the roles that are socially acceptable for their respective genders.[4] These expectations, a form of gender stereotyping, dictate what society sees as suitable behaviors for men versus what is suitable for women. This includes women taking positions of lower power, having the bulk of the responsibility for domestic tasks in relationships, and the idea that men and women have different occupational roles based on their psychological and physiological characteristics.

Social Role Theory contends that all psychological differences can be attributed to expectations of gender and cultural standards rather than biological factors.[5] It builds on the think-manager-think-male framework.[6] This psychological phenomenon is very well known and exists because the traits we typically associate with leaders—forceful, dominant, strong, competent, even heroic—are stereotypically associated with men. This framework analyzes the role of male leadership and dominates leadership literature.[7]

In the late 1970s, psychologist Virginia Schein completed a series of experiments that indicated that both male and female managers viewed management positions as masculine and better fitted for males.[8] That study reflected its time, meaning that those indications reflect the culture and socioeconomic status of women during the early 1970s. As times changed, so did ideologies.

Contemporary authors argue that responses from female managers starting in the twentieth century no longer display such stereotypical views. Reactions from female managers in later studies show women's belief that both male and female managers possess traits that can make them successful leaders.

The change in thinking is attributable to the view of leadership roles among women and changes in social functions. In the early twentieth century, women began to aggressively challenge men in the labor force, sparking a change in the viewpoint regarding women and leadership. A shift occurred in the female perspective but not the male.[9] Thus, gender-biased perceptions of female leadership ability continue to be prominent within leadership theory.

Like Role Congruity Theory, Social Role Theory is grounded in gender bias and stereotypes. We still live in a climate of male dominance in leadership, and this theory assumes that characteristics associated with male leadership reign supreme over those widely accepted for females. It further explains the restrictive mindset women leaders and their aspiring protégés encounter.

Social Role Theory explains why society tells women to "stay in their lane." As women, we must first be cognizant of where this attitude comes from so that we can redirect its power toward mending gender inequities.

THE FAIRY TALE—HOW SOCIAL ROLE THEORY PLAYS OUT IN OUR CULTURAL BELIEFS

Society is still pushing the "glass slipper" notion.

The fairy-tale portrayal of marriage has been a cultural norm for centuries. Stories and movies often depict marriage as the ultimate happy ending where two people fall in love, get married, and live happily ever after. While marriage can certainly be a beautiful and fulfilling experience for many people, it is important to recognize that real-life marriages can be much more complicated than the idealized fairy-tale version.

Marriage involves two unique individuals with their own sets of values, goals, and personalities who come together to form a partnership. This partnership requires effort, communication, compromise, and a willingness to work through difficult times. Not all marriages are perfect.

Furthermore, the fairy-tale portrayal of marriage often reinforces gender stereotypes. Women are depicted as passive princesses waiting for their prince charming to rescue them, and men as the dominant saviors. This kind of portrayal places unrealistic expectations on both men and women and can perpetuate unhealthy power dynamics in relationships.

While the fairy-tale version of marriage can be a romantic idea, it is important to approach marriage with realistic expectations and recognize that it requires effort, commitment, and communication to create a healthy and fulfilling partnership.

In addition to approaching marriage with realistic expectations, we must acknowledge the concepts learned from Social Role Theory on our understanding of gender roles in relationships. Social Role Theory suggests that gender roles are shaped by cultural norms and expectations, which can influence how individuals behave in their relationships.

For as long as I can remember, traditional gender roles dictate that men are the breadwinners, and women should be caregivers and fulfill domestic duties. These expectations create imbalances in power dynamics and lead to conflict and dissatisfaction in relationships.

Not everyone fits into the mold where men fill certain roles, and so do women. Not every woman wants to cook, clean, have babies, and take care of the home. That's not to say that carrying out domestic duties lacks importance. Those duties are arguably extremely important. However, many women desire more. Running businesses motivates them. Rather than waiting for the man to bring home the money, some women today prefer to collaborate with men on the job and share strategies and earnings with their significant others. For the great majority of women today, being restricted to female gender roles stifles their contribution to the marriage partnership. To create a healthy and fulfilling partnership, we must continue to challenge and break down traditional gender roles and expectations. Both partners should have equal opportunities and responsibilities in the relationship, including decision-making and domestic tasks. By recognizing and addressing the impact limiting thoughts explained by Social Role Theory on our understanding of gender roles in relationships, we can create more equitable and fulfilling marriage partnerships.

Marriage, despite its timeless allure, is continually evolving, reshaped by shifting societal norms and changing dynamics. Yet it remains profoundly impacted by how gender roles are perceived and negotiated within the institution.

CRASH-LANDING BIAS—GLASS CLIFF THEORY

If asked about a challenging situation we had to take charge of and work through, you and I could probably state the problem, what needed to be done, and the steps we took to solve it. In all honesty, we could probably talk about several because life constantly presents difficult and even demanding times we must navigate.

Women are more than capable of handling tough situations—that's a well-known fact. Sometimes, our ability to do so is called upon during inopportune times for us as leaders. Glass Cliff Theory speaks to this fact. The Glass Cliff refers to the phenomenon whereby women are more likely than men to be appointed to leadership positions in times when they are expected to fail.[10] As a result, these women are more subject to criticism because these positions involve leading during a time of crisis.

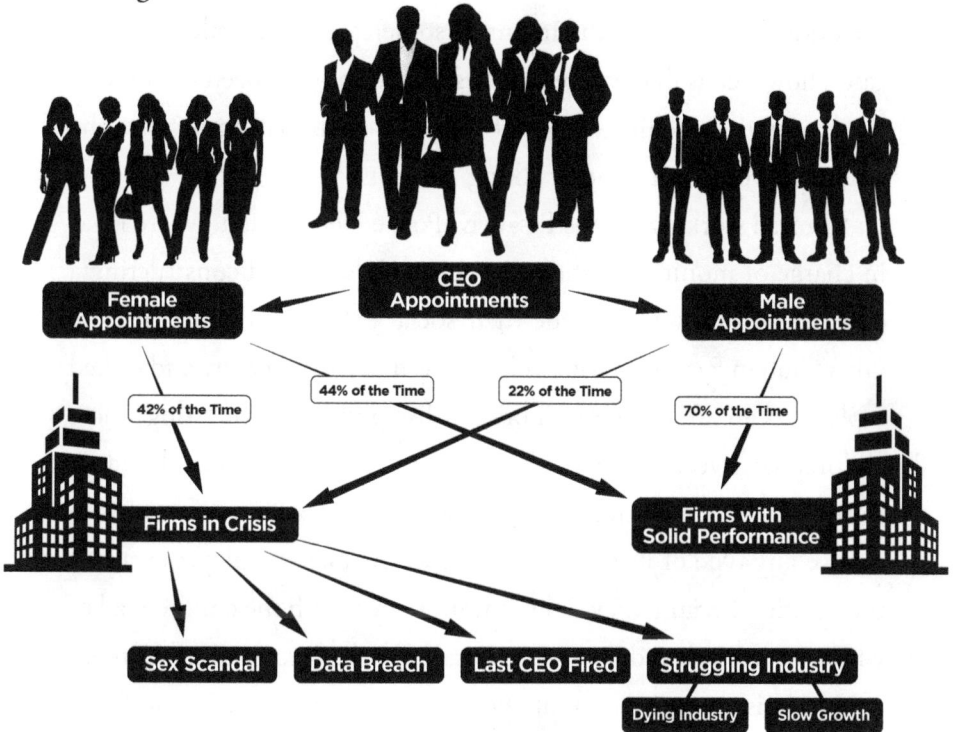

This phenomenon holds that women are promoted to senior roles due to societal perceptions of the leadership attributes they bring to a crisis.[11] Women are perceived as better equipped to handle conflict because society deems their leadership style as more nurturing. At first thought, we might think that this is a compliment to what women bring to the leadership role, but that is not the case. The gender biases described by this theory explain inequities in the workplace including workload, sexism, lack of access to social networks, and other direct and indirect forms of discrimination and bias.[12]

Finally, a theory that recognizes the positive attributes of women leaders, right? Not necessarily. The Glass Cliff operates under the guise of "appropriately" promoting women to effectively lead the way during intensely difficult and critical situations. Some people may think of it as an opportunity for women to successfully lead against the odds. That may be the intent in some cases. The reality in most cases, however, is that women in these positions have been set up with the expectation to fail. Glass Cliff Theory pays special attention to the failure of women in senior-ranking positions.[13]

I recall working for the Pasadena Police Department, where I was in charge of monitoring the activities of children and constructing a curriculum that would guide their social behaviors for the Boys & Girls Club in Pasadena. The children lived in the inner city and lacked a place to go after school. Short on discipline and parenting, these children were very challenging. I understood the huge task of building relationships and getting them to focus and be still long enough to receive any type of instruction. None of the male employees wanted the position because they did not want to deal with the children, all of whom were Black and brown. So I was offered a "promotion." Lurking behind this promotion crept the concepts mentioned in the Glass Cliff Theory. Was it only because I, as a woman, was suitable for this leadership situation requiring crisis management? Was I being set up to fail? Regardless, I accepted the task to go in, create a curriculum, and implement it within the club. It was hard; believe me. There were times when I felt like quitting, but as I looked into the faces of all the Black and brown children, being as undisciplined as they may have been, I refused to give up. The end result may not have been ideal, but I was able to create a sense of unity by introducing activities that spoke their language that they could identify with. Not only did I deal with the challenge head-on, but I also made a positive impact on the lives of young people.

POINT OF REFLECTION

Reflecting on Glass Cliff Theory, consider how perceptions of leadership opportunities and challenges may differ based on gender. Have you ever observed instances where women were appointed to leadership positions during times of crisis? How did societal expectations and biases influence perceptions of their leadership potential and the likelihood of success or failure in those roles? Furthermore, how can awareness of the Glass Cliff phenomenon inform efforts to promote gender equality and inclusive leadership practices?

Still Bossing Up

One recent example of the Glass Cliff is the appointment of Kamala Harris as the first female and first Black vice president of the United States. While her appointment is historic, it also placed her in a precarious position as she took office during a difficult time. She began the position while we lived in the midst of political and social turmoil, including the COVID-19 pandemic, economic instability, and racial justice protests.

Research on the Glass Cliff suggests that women and minorities are more likely to be appointed to leadership positions in times of crisis when the risk of failure is higher. This phenomenon can be seen as a way for organizations to signal their commitment to diversity and inclusivity, while also shifting blame for potential failures onto the individuals appointed to these positions.

Harris's appointment to the vice presidency exemplifies the Glass Cliff phenomenon because she assumed a position of power during a time of significant uncertainty and risk. Being the first woman and person of color in this role, Harris faced heightened scrutiny, criticism, and the expectation to navigate a complex and demanding political landscape.

Despite these challenges, Harris continues to demonstrate her leadership skills and commitment to creating positive change. Her appointment has been seen as a significant step forward for gender and racial equity in the United States. However, her position also underscores the need for us to continue addressing the barriers women and minorities face in leadership positions. Efforts to promote greater inclusivity and equity in all aspects of society must continue.

Role Congruity, Social Role, and Glass Cliff Theories help us to better understand how male dominance influences social constructs that act as barriers to women's leadership in Western culture.

Social Role Theory suggests that societal norms shape the roles that men and women play in society, leading to gender stereotypes and expectations that can limit women's potential. Role Congruity Theory suggests that women's success in leadership positions may be undermined by a perceived mismatch between the qualities that society associates with leadership and those that are stereotypically associated with women. Glass Cliff Theory suggests that women are more likely to be appointed to leadership positions during times of crisis or turmoil, when the chances of failure are higher, making it more difficult to succeed.

These theories emerge from observed patterns in society, indicating that they are, to a significant extent, influenced by prevailing social norms. Thus, it can be argued that social norms initially inform the development of theories, which subsequently reinforce, critique, or attempt to alter these norms. This dynamic interaction means that theories and social norms are mutually influential.

By being aware of these theories and the societal expectations they represent, we can work to break down gender stereotypes and challenge their limiting assumptions. This can be done through mentorship, advocacy, and networking, as well as by promoting policies that support women's advancement and create a more inclusive workplace culture.

Ultimately, it is crucial not to ignore or deny the societal forces that shape women's opportunities and experiences in the workplace. I get it. In a civilized society, rules, norms, and order are indispensable. They serve as the backbone of our social fabric, guiding our interactions and establishing standards of behavior that uphold peace, harmony, and mutual respect. Without these guidelines, chaos could easily ensue, leading to discord and conflict.

While rules, norms, and order are essential for maintaining social cohesion and stability, however, they can also inadvertently perpetuate inequalities and biases, as explained by theories such as Social Role Theory, Role Congruity Theory, and Glass Cliff Theory.

In this way, while rules and norms are intended to maintain order and stability, they can also serve as barriers to equality and inclusion when influenced by biased perceptions and stereotypes. Recognizing and challenging these biases is essential for creating a more equitable society where individuals are judged based on their abilities and potential rather than outdated societal norms.

And now that the three theories have been explained, we will explore a bit deeper by looking at social norms and systems that these theories support.

CHAPTER 2

Perceptions of Emotion and Leadership Ability

A strong woman looks a challenge dead in the eye and gives it a wink.

—GINA CAREY

POINT OF REFLECTION

"Women are more emotional than men." I have heard this statement and encountered the same mindset more times than I care to count. It permeates our society because it is one of the most influential gender stereotypes in Western culture.

As leaders, women must walk a tightrope to maintain the perception of power. Research on the tightrope of emotion describes how women's expression of emotion presents a fundamental barrier to their ability to climb ranks and succeed as leaders.[14] In her study "Leading with Their Hearts? How Gender Stereotypes of Emotion Lead to Biased Evaluations of Female Leaders," Victoria L. Brescoll explores how gender stereotypes influence perceptions of leadership effectiveness, particularly focusing on the emotional expectations and biases that affect women's leadership roles. The study explains the nature of gender-emotion stereotypes. Examination of this research reveals that society has gendered beliefs that women are more emotional than men.[15]

Just because women show more emotions does not mean men are less emotional. In fact, the same study shows that men and women do not differ substantially in the extent to which they experience emotion, just in the degree to which they outwardly express emotions to others. Unfortunately, women are subjected to different rules, labeled as unable to control the outward display of emotion, and viewed as less capable of controlling how emotions influence them. Interestingly, this study challenges the belief that emotion brings about irrational thinking into decision-making.[16]

The consequence of this biased belief depicts us as ineffective leaders. Society views our decision-making behaviors as influenced by emotion and therefore irrational, lacking objectivity, biased, unstable, unpredictable, and sentimental. Gender stereotypes of emotion present obstacles to our ability as women to effectively lead others. The stereotype of emotion and its relationship to gender-biased perceptions of women's leadership ability hinders the growth in the number of women reaching upper echelons of leadership.

Once upon a time, the inside of the home was considered the best place for women's "emotional" leadership. It made sense for women to provide emotional support that structured and stabilized the home. Their historical roles as nurturing caretakers shaped the division of labor within the family unit, and it became the norm for women to take care of the home. However, fulfillment of these roles morphed into a hindrance for modern-day women who pursue leadership opportunities outside of their homes.

Though it is considered an archaic practice by some, the division of labor in the family continues to impede our access to leadership positions. Numerous studies show that the number of children has the most substantial marginal effect on the likelihood of women becoming CEOs.[17] Women step out of their careers to take care of children and family more often than men. This is consistent with findings that the division of labor within the family continues to have a high degree of influence on our appointments to high-level positions.

BY THE NUMBERS

"Women in the Workplace 2019," the largest study of the state of women in corporate America, confirms the issue regarding women in leadership. Based on five years of data from almost six hundred companies, the 2019 report indicated the following:

- Women are less likely to be hired and promoted to manager. For every one hundred men promoted and hired to manager, only seventy-two women are promoted and hired.
- Men hold 62 percent of manager-level positions, while women hold just 38 percent. The number of women decreases at every subsequent level.
- One-third of companies set gender representation targets for first-level manager roles, compared to 41 percent for senior levels of management.
- We can add one million more women to management in corporate America over the next five years if women are hired and promoted to manager at the same rate as men.[18]

These statistics display the blatant disparity of women in leadership roles. It is commonplace and has changed very slowly over time, so it does not represent the pool of talented women. Levels of management represent leadership opportunities. Whether the numbers are analyzed by looking at numerical values or percentages, leadership opportunities for females clearly lag behind that of our male counterparts. Based on the sheer number of women holding advanced degrees in business, coupled with substantial hands-on management experience and the drive and leadership skills to run Fortune 500 companies, these numbers reveal how powerful theories, social perceptions, and, most of all, male organizational culture control and influence women's access to leadership status.

In no way do these numbers define who we are as leaders. They do not represent our competence as bosses. We are more than capable of leading with leveled emotion and skill to unite and drive organizations and teams.

FLIPPING THE SCRIPT—USING EMOTION TO OUR ADVANTAGE

Flipping the script means turning a situation around or looking at it from a different perspective. In the context of using emotions to our advantage, this would mean recognizing the positive aspects of emotions, rather than viewing them as a weakness.

Emotions can be a powerful tool for individuals, both consciously and unconsciously. Emotions can help people connect with others, express themselves, and empathize with those around them. Here are some examples of how emotions can be used to our advantage:

1. Building relationships: Expressing emotions helps build strong connections with others. When we show vulnerability and express our emotions, it can help others feel more comfortable opening up to us in return. This can help build trust and deepen our relationships.

2. Communicating effectively: Emotions can be a powerful tool for communication. When we express our emotions, it can help others understand how we feel and what is important to us. This can help us communicate more effectively, both in personal and professional contexts.

3. Motivating action: Emotions can be a powerful motivator for action. When we feel strongly about something, it can inspire us to act and make positive changes in our lives and the lives of those around us.

4. Inspiring creativity: Emotions can also inspire creativity. When we are feeling strong emotions, it can help us tap into our creativity and come up with new ideas and solutions to problems.

By flipping the script and recognizing the positive aspects of emotions, we can use them to our advantage. Emotions can be a powerful tool for building relationships, communicating effectively, motivating action, and inspiring creativity.

NORMS OF MALE ORGANIZATIONAL CULTURE

Think about the basic definition of male organizational culture. Male organizational culture reflects the values, beliefs, and norms that characterize an organization with a heavily male-dominated population.[19] This definition suggests that organizational culture reflects what is common, typical, and general for the organization.

Some studies suggest that the obstacle to equal representation of women revolves around male models of leadership and norms of male organizational culture.[20] Therefore, traits typically assigned to men, such as ambition, competitiveness, aggression, and control, are appreciated. On the other hand, there is less appreciation for more communal traits such as empathy, kindness, or concern for others, as these traits are considered "feminine." Society considers senior management positions as "masculine." This gender-biased thinking is responsible for the broad imbalance of women in senior executive-level positions.

A study by Avigail Moor, Ayala Cohen, and Ortal Beeri titled "In Quest of Excellence, Not Power: Women's Paths to Positions of Influence and Leadership" delved into the impact of male organizational culture on the representation of women in senior executive-level positions.[21] The research highlighted how traits traditionally associated with men, such as ambition, competitiveness, and control, are valued and rewarded within male-dominated organizational cultures. Conversely, traits considered more communal or "feminine," such as empathy and kindness, are often overlooked or undervalued. The study found that women aspiring to senior leadership roles often feel pressured to adopt more "masculine" qualities to overcome these biases and barriers.

As women attain senior-level leadership positions, we feel forced to adopt more "masculine" qualities to bypass this obstacle. In the absence of a suitable mechanism that would enable us to combine career and family optimally, male organizational culture presents an additional barrier whereby we must make concessions in our family makeup. The unequal standard of higher expectations remains elusive for our respective male counterparts. Not only must we walk and talk as confident and competent individuals in our specific areas, but we must also understand and assimilate to a norm unnatural for who we are. This is how we attain and maintain higher ranks in government and corporate America. Clearly, this is above and beyond what men are expected to do within the comfort of the male-dominated climate.

THE OLD BOY NETWORK

The "Old Boy Network" sounds harmless. In some cases, it just might be. But let us understand exactly what it is and how it affects people within an organization. The network itself is an informal male social system. It purposely excludes less-dominant men and women from membership to band together and preserve the upper ranks as a predominantly male domain.[22]

This informal social system originates in early-childhood experiences for boys and was found to have a bearing on the appointment of men and women to executive leadership positions.[23] In other words, childhood experiences influence disparities between the genders, subsequently impacting men's and women's leadership preparation and success.

We should take a closer look at childhood and how it affects gender positions later in life. Sociologist Pierre Bourdieu explains that early childhood and adolescence are peak times for developing gendered behavior passively acquired by observing societal norms.[24] In other words, children pick up on gender roles by watching what goes on in society. For instance, certain childhood environments provide boys with opportunities to take risks, exercise independence, and achieve success. These experiences foster self-confidence in males, influencing their attitudes toward risk-taking in adulthood. The different treatment of boys and girls around taking risks in childhood play promotes less self-confidence and self-esteem for women as they mature.[25] Shyness is more socially acceptable for female children, but reinforcing this behavior happens at the expense of self-confidence and assertive behaviors.[26] Additionally, games that boys traditionally play, such as football and other full-contact team sports, contribute to the development of "resilience, leadership, strategic thinking, and an understanding of the importance of social capital."[27]

The Bourdieusian framework considers learned capabilities as valuable capital. Embodied understanding is more than merely conceptual understanding. It encompasses our most basic way of being in and engaging with our surroundings in a profound, visceral manner.[28] In this case, capital is defined as "all goods, material and symbolic, without distinction, that present themselves as rare and worthy of being sought after in a particular social formation."[29] This capital is attained through life experiences and social expectations that shape roles and behaviors toward each gender group.[30]

Interestingly, the Bourdieusian framework describes how this valuable capital allows for the domination of one group of individuals, namely male leaders, to intergenerationally reproduce views about useful capital without widespread resistance.[31] These individuals can designate what valuable capital is required and the preferred situation in which it is generated. In male-dominated executive and CEO roles, powers that hinder women from obtaining valuable combinations of capital are primarily responsible for the unequal representation of women reaching executive status.

Gendered patterns in the accumulation of career-relevant experiences stretch back to birth. These gender-related early-childhood experiences are a significant contributor to society's perception of male and female leadership ability. So much of this framework remains to be explored, and it will be further discussed in chapter 2. The Bourdieusian framework may be novel to many but remains a valuable source for understanding how social constructs and experiences influence behavior of each gender. It also gives insight into how that influenced behavior enables individuals to navigate the exclusive Old Boy Network.

POINT OF REFLECTION

Reflecting on the concept of the Old Boy Network and its influence on gender disparities in leadership, consider the role of childhood experiences in shaping societal perceptions of gender roles. Have you ever observed or experienced gendered patterns in childhood environments that contribute to disparities in confidence, self-esteem, and leadership preparation later in life? How do societal norms and expectations around gendered behavior in childhood impact individuals' opportunities and attitudes toward risk-taking, assertiveness, and leadership as adults? Furthermore, how can understanding these early influences inform efforts to promote gender equality and inclusivity in leadership and organizational cultures?

Still Bossing Up

Women are actively fighting against the Old Boy Network in a number of ways. One approach is the establishment of our own networks and support systems, which provide access to opportunities, mentorship, and advocacy. These networks provide a platform for us to share our experiences, raise awareness of the challenges we face, and push for greater inclusivity and equity in the workplace and beyond.

Another approach is women challenging gender stereotypes and biases directly, through initiatives such as unconscious bias training, diversity and inclusion programs, and advocacy for policies that promote gender equity. We are also increasingly speaking out about experiences of discrimination and bias, using social media and other platforms to share our stories and raise awareness of the challenges we face.

In addition, more of us are taking on leadership roles in a variety of fields and using our positions to advocate for greater gender equity and inclusivity. This includes pushing for policies that promote equal pay, parental leave, and flexible work arrangements, as well as advocating for greater representation of women and minorities.

SHADOW BOXING

Our fight against the Old Boy Network is apparent, and progress has been made. However, there is still much work to be done to ensure that all individuals have equal opportunities to succeed, regardless of their gender or background.

The exclusivity of the Old Boy Network puts up walls to keep out individuals deemed unworthy of entry. It excludes some men due to their lack of social and educational status. Unfortunately, lack of social status and educational opportunities tends to follow individuals and families from one generation to the next, and even more so for women. Education is what we know, whereas social capital refers to who we know. The saying, "It's not what you know. It's who you know," captures this concept.

For hundreds of years, limited education and access to certain social advantages congested our feminine paths with various obstructions. We continue to navigate roadblocks by attaining advanced college degrees and jump hurdles by conforming to unnatural and uncomfortable male-dominated culture only to face the walls of the Old Boy Network. Yet we are still bossing up!

UNPACKING MALE GROUPTHINK

You don't have to play masculine to be a strong woman.
—MARY ELIZABETH WINSTEAD

If you look at the word "groupthink," you might come to the conclusion that it simply means what a set of people believes or expects. *Psychology Today* states the following:

> Groupthink occurs when a group of well-intentioned people make irrational or non-optimal decisions spurred by the urge to conform or the discouragement of dissent. This problematic or premature consensus may be fueled by a particular agenda or simply because group members value harmony and coherence above rational thinking. In the interest of making a decision that furthers their group cause, members may ignore any ethical or moral consequences.[32]

Again, this has to do with men thinking that women should occupy certain positions and not be included in things that are historically male dominated. Long-established organizational culture assumes men to be the leaders. Because of this, men believe leadership comes naturally to them.

The division of labor at home has a lot to do with this thinking. For the most part, women cook, clean, and raise the children. A majority of men continue to believe that certain roles are gender specific. However, there is a noticeable and dramatic shift in this thinking in the millennial mindset. Millennial women are not so easily signing up for domestic duty. More than ever before, men stay at home and equally share in domestic labor.

For our discussion, male groupthink will focus on how men as a group believe that women should hold certain positions in society or in organizations because of gender. As of right now, male groupthink is the sign of the times for men of certain generations.

As women, however, we can stand in our own truth and not be concerned with male groupthink. Ignoring its existence is the only way to remove it as an obstacle. Ignore its presence, and thereby extinguish its power!

Still Bossing Up

One real-life example of how women are fighting against male groupthink is in the field of technology. Historically, the technology industry has been dominated by men, and many of the products and services developed have reflected the perspectives and biases of this male-dominated culture.

In recent years, however, women in technology have been working to challenge these assumptions and promote greater diversity and inclusivity in the industry. For example, groups such as Women Who Code and Girls Who Code have been established to provide support, mentorship, and training for women and girls who are interested in pursuing careers in technology. I call them boss groups. They see the need for necessary change and build a coalition to make the change happen.

We have a place in the field of technology. Thus, women in the field have also been advocating for greater representation and inclusivity in the design and development of technology products and services. This includes pushing for more diverse teams and perspectives, as well as for greater consideration of the ways in which technology can impact different groups of people.

As a result of these efforts, there has been increasing recognition of the importance of diversity and inclusivity in technology, and many companies are now making efforts to promote greater representation and inclusivity in their teams and products. While there is still much work to be done, these efforts demonstrate the ways in which women are fighting against male groupthink and working to create a more equitable and inclusive technology industry.

REAL TALK

Mindsets that bind include societal representations limiting our entry to leadership and societal practices hindering our professional advancement. Role Congruity Theory, Social Role Theory, and Glass Cliff Theory stand as prominent theories intricately linked to the obstacles we as women face in our journey toward leadership advancement in Western culture. These theories create situations in which we have to make choices that have negative results no matter what—situations referred to as double binds.

A behavioral double bind is described as "a behavioral norm that creates a situation where a person cannot win no matter what she does."[33] One study describes emotional double binds as the need for women to "walk a line" between expressing enough but not too much emotion to avoid the risk of violating stereotypes.[34] Double binds limit our ability to display a full range of behaviors.[35]

Norms of male organizational culture permeated a huge portion of my career. Most companies that I have ever worked for chose a white male figure as the head of most departments. Men made most corporate decisions. Back then the Old Boy Network was very strong and united, and if you were not a white man, you just could not mingle with them. Whenever I exercised leadership ability, I found myself always having to choose between the lesser of two evils—criticized for being too strong or mocked for being too timid. Double binds penetrated most of my early- and mid-career.

Throughout history, double binds have been used to usurp our power. For example, we are challenged to speak assertively but criticized if we speak *too* assertively. We are judged for being too feminine and negatively viewed if we are perceived as too masculine. Self-promotion, decisiveness, warmth, and selflessness are all manners of communication expressed freely by men but considered unacceptable behaviors for us.

In the sphere of corporate governance, the presence of gender diversity is crucial to reducing the impact of double binds on organizational cultures. You will find these behavioral double binds resonating throughout our discussion. Here is the unfortunate part: double binds symbolize a subtle form of gender bias against women that poses a formidable challenge in terms of identifying and implementing effective ways to eliminate them.

Mindsets that bind are the "rock and the hard place" for women. Contemplating exactly how to handle a matter at hand becomes quite a task. Our quandary includes thoughts such as whether or not we should inflect confidence in our voices when we speak up about a situation. Should we "speak from our chest"? Then, we think maybe not because that might give the impression that we are too assertive or even borderline confrontational.

Perhaps we should just choose our battles, avoid voicing concerns, and allow certain situations to work themselves out. Taking that route might make us seem indecisive and too passive to fulfill executive leadership roles. Sometimes we simply do not know whether to act in one manner or the other. Therein lies our dilemma and the crux of mindsets that bind us.

BOSS MOVES—NOT NECESSARILY SO

Perhaps the obvious should have been acknowledged from the outset. Men and women are different. Physically, socially, emotionally, etc.— men and women operate and interact in different ways. The in-depth exploration and discussion within this chapter give a candid viewpoint of how those differences are used to frame social perspectives and roles for men and women.

Many in our society still subscribe to the theory that women are born as nurturers, mothers who raise children, and therefore better suited for certain professional roles in society. Even in the twenty-first century, we still struggle with these same biases and prejudices. We still face the constant tug of war for corporate and political positioning with "the good old boys." There are groups that consciously exclude women solely on the basis of gender. Consequently, we try fixing ourselves to fit into the male-dominated culture that currently prevails.

Fitting in a male-dominated culture will not happen easily for us. Conversations among men naturally differ from those of women. Men often engage in conversations that women might consider sexist or degrading. In cases like this, we should accept and find comfort with not being included. However, some of us still play into roles just to fit in. We try to force ourselves to fit into situations so that we can be included. This is futile. Based on research, female acceptance into heavily dominated male careers, clubs, professional societies, and organizations is virtually nonexistent.[36]

Like any dominant subculture, the Old Boy Network has a lot to lose if its culture is forced to change and invite female entrants.[37] If large numbers of women rose to top positions in large corporations, it is quite probable they would challenge the prevailing masculine cultural norms the same way they did when they infiltrated other areas of corporate life. Research confirms this.

An influx of females would question the need to hide or eliminate emotions in the workplace. The use of sports metaphors and the importance of golf would likely be challenged.[45] "Why do we need to hide how we feel?" might be a prevailing question. "What does golf have to do with our roles in the organization?" could possibly be posed. Both questions would undoubtedly confront the culture.

Attempting to alter a male-dominated organization entrenched in a rigid mindset into the desired state is an exercise in futility. It is at this point that women often encounter a metaphorical ceiling, despite their persistent efforts to challenge and break through the confines of an inflexible culture. For hundreds of years, gender-based prejudices and stereotypes have emerged to form one-sided norms, systems, and mindsets that bind us.

There is so much forward movement happening and more on the brink of taking place that we must continue persevering and preparing for the best. Collectively, we are not only resisting norms, systems, and mindsets that bind, but we are also forging through. As we forge through, let us embrace who we are naturally and resist the pressure to give up our innate abilities or belittle our femininity.

LAYING THE GROUNDWORK

In this chapter, we addressed the foundational problems that create ties that bind women to societal opinions and social constructs. This understanding is critical for the journey of enlightenment that we are undertaking. As we evolve into our natural place in society as sheroes, understanding the headwinds we will face will help us to change the trajectory to one more conducive to our success.

This foundational information is essential for current and aspiring women leaders. It clarifies the obstacles and their origination. Equipped with this knowledge, we can stop trying to navigate these obstacles. Instead, we can begin ignoring the "noise" seeking to distract us, cutting our own paths, and creating our own opportunities.

In the words of the 2019 "Women in the Workplace" study, "The broken rung is the biggest obstacle women face."[38] We may not be able to change the societal perception of women, but we can change our approach to creating opportunities for each other by building our own ladders one rung at a time. The first rung of that ladder includes an honest self-reflection and collective reflection on what we might be doing to exacerbate or fall prey to the mindsets that bind.

MOVING FORWARD

We acknowledge mindsets that bind for the reality they are but continue to move forward toward cultivating and building upon our own potential. Thus, the discussion in the next chapter is imperative.

In the next chapter, we examine how women may contribute to gender bias and negative perceptions of our own strength and resilience. We will take a closer look at current and past situations that reveal how we unconsciously fall into stereotypical traps.

CHAPTER 3

The Traps

I am not afraid of storms, for I am learning how to sail my ship.
—LOUISA MAY ALCOTT

I am impassioned by the dilemma I see women in today that traps them into societal norms. Because of the subconscious effects of societal entrapment, potential lies dormant in many women. Somewhere along the way in my personal evolution, I realized that all humans have the potential for growth and development. I also came to realize that undernourished capabilities are relatively nonexistent. Capabilities that have fallen into the trap of societal expectations and are seemingly absent will not thrive.

A powerful example of a woman who broke free from these societal constraints is Malala Yousafzai. Despite facing extreme adversity, including an assassination attempt by the Taliban at just fifteen years old, Malala refused to succumb to the oppressive norms that sought to silence her. Instead, she became a fierce advocate for girls' education around the world, demonstrating that her voice and intelligence were her true sources of power, not her appearance. Through her unwavering commitment to change, she not only reclaimed her narrative but also inspired millions of girls globally to pursue their education and dreams, proving that breaking free from societal expectations can lead to remarkable achievements and transformative impacts. Malala's journey exemplifies the strength and potential that lies within every woman, waiting to be unleashed when she rejects conforming roles and embraces her true self.

A planted seed will not grow without water and sunlight, but when the sun is allowed to shine on that planted seed, and the rain waters that seed, chances of its germination and growth are highly probable. As sheroes, our sun and water come from within. We are all capable of growing and thriving. We cannot allow our dreams to be voided by societal perceptions!

At a pivotal point in my personal journey, a profound sense of gratitude came over me. It was gratitude that motivated me to ignore societal expectations and challenge myself beyond perceived limitations. This gratitude was not merely an isolated feeling; it was inspired by the incredible women I had shared my experiences with during that transformative weekend in the mountains. As we sat together, sharing our vulnerabilities, triumphs, and the weight of societal expectations, I found strength in their stories. This newfound appreciation motivated me to challenge myself beyond the limitations I had once accepted. While I faced stumbling blocks and made plenty of mistakes along the way, the motivation I received from these remarkable women propelled me forward. I learned to embrace each fall as an opportunity to rise again, always leaning on that sense of community to push me toward progress and a deeper understanding of what I could achieve. From that pivotal moment, when I fell, I always tried to fall forward.

Recognizing that my greatest weapon against societal constraints was my capacity for critical thinking and rationality, I felt that education was the key. I pursued and achieved my bachelor's, master's, and doctorate degrees. During this pursuit, my personal life continued to unfold. I experienced the joys of marriage, the blessings of motherhood with two children, the pain of divorce, and the audacity to uproot my entire existence and move from California to Texas.

I share these personal experiences and anecdotes not only as a testament to my journey of self-discovery and empowerment, but also to instill hope within a society of women who, at some point, may have veered off course under the influence of detrimental ideologies. It's essential to remember that it's okay to lose our way sometimes, as it often leads us to a path better suited for our growth. Unfortunately, these detours can often be a direct result of malevolent forces that perpetuate harmful ideologies, forcing us to question our worth and capabilities. However, with each passing day, it becomes glaringly apparent that these aberrant influences crumble under the penetrating light of truth: the truth that we are powerful, resilient, and capable of anything we set our minds to. As sheroes, we're not only bossing up individually, but we're also collectively shedding light on these detrimental influences and empowering each other to stand tall. In this chapter I aim to enable the light of truth to shine brightly through the darkness of potential entrapment.

PAUSE AND POWER UP

Placing the blame for our plight in society often offers a convenience that spares us from confronting our own responsibilities. While we are not accountable for the origins of social constructs or the barriers they impose, it is vital to acknowledge that we do possess the capacity to respond. The pivotal question arises: "How can we respond effectively to foster progress toward our goals?" The answer lies in self-reflection and evaluation. By critically assessing the psychological impacts of restrictive social norms, systems, and constructs that limit our potential, we can better understand their effects on our lives. These evaluations—coupled with an honest appraisal of our reactions—lay the foundation for intentional changes in our responses. While acknowledging these external pressures is crucial, it is equally important to recognize where to place this "blame." We cannot control the establishment of societal constructs or the barriers they create, but we can control our responses and choices.

So some may ask, "How can we respond to make progressive steps toward our goals?" The short answer is to reflect and evaluate. Once we evaluate the psychological effects of those restrictive social norms, systems, and ties that bind us and note our responses for the purpose of altering our outcome, we will be on the path to making progress despite social conditioning and societal limitations.

Pavlov's dog experiments played a critical role in the discovery of one of the most important concepts in psychology: classical conditioning.[39] Classical conditioning places great emphasis on the significance of environmental influence and highlights the power of nurture in shaping our behaviors. When society establishes an unhealthy norm, it elicits an equally unhealthy response.

Throughout this chapter, I extend a warm invitation for you to engage in a profound discussion on how we almost instinctively confine ourselves within societal expectations, all due to our own patterns of thinking. In order to delve deeper into this discourse, we will explore the Bourdieusian framework, which provides a valuable lens through which to understand this phenomenon.

As we delve deeper into the invisible forces that women face, the shero narrative unfolds with even greater power. The concepts we have just discussed have real-world implications for women, and as the journey of the shero continues to evolve, so do the situations we encounter.

Sadly, women all too often find themselves ensnared in psychological traps. According to the Cambridge Dictionary, a trap is a dreadful predicament where escape seems impossible. As women, we frequently find ourselves competing to overcome societal inequities and disprove stereotypes. We are trapped in a cycle of constantly striving to prove ourselves and break free from restricting societal constructs. Consider a woman in a corporate environment striving for a leadership role. She may feel pressured to conform to traditional standards of professionalism, often facing the dual burden of proving her competence while also contending with biases that undermine her capabilities. This cycle not only reinforces the very stereotypes she aims to dismantle but can also lead to burnout and self-doubt. This cycle makes us fall into the very inequities we are attempting to conquer. However, there are ways to break free from this bewildering entrapment.

POINT OF REFLECTION

Reflecting on societal expectations reveals how deeply they can unconsciously impact our behavior and decisions. From an early age, these expectations become intertwined with our sense of self, shaping what we consider proper and acceptable behavior. For example, I have noticed how ingrained beliefs about leadership and assertiveness have influenced my professional approach. The traditional view that women should be nurturing and agreeable often conflicts with the qualities associated with leadership, presenting unique challenges in my career. Additionally, social conditioning shapes our ideas of beauty and success, steering us toward ideals that may not truly resonate with us. This influence is evident in our consumer habits, time management, and task prioritization.

However, recognizing these patterns empowers us to consider new perspectives and possibilities. By understanding how social conditioning affects our lives, we can start to explore paths that align more closely with our true selves, paving the way for a more fulfilling existence. What societal expectations have influenced your behavior, and how can you begin recognizing and evaluating these influences to enhance your authentic life journey?

DEEP DIVE

As women, we often find ourselves caught in a cycle of direct competition with men, striving to prove our worth and capabilities in an attempt to counter deep-seated stereotypes. However, engaging in this competitive mindset may not be the most effective approach. It requires a significant amount of energy and focus to continually nullify the negative perceptions ingrained in the collective consciousness.

Instead of trying to prove ourselves within the confines of these biased expectations, we should redirect our energy toward embracing our unique strengths and qualities as women leaders. By shifting our focus toward nurturing and leveraging our innate talents, we can carve our own paths to success. It is through authenticity and embracing our diverse perspectives that we can create meaningful change and challenge the traditional notions of leadership.

So rather than getting caught up in the energy-draining cycle of disproving stereotypes, let us channel our efforts to building supportive networks, fostering collaboration, and amplifying our voices. Together, we can shape a future where our leadership is recognized and valued based on merit and contribution, rather than conforming to societal expectations.

Gender-biased traps are hard not to fall into if we are constantly trying to avoid them. Trying to prove that our skills are just as good if not better than men's is a job in itself. Men's innate DNA and skill set prepare them to excel in situations that society deems more suitable for the masculine of the species. Therefore, it is a fixed fight when women try to combat that stereotype. It is a fight that cannot be won; women literally cannot compete with men in certain areas because of physiological and psychological makeup. Our structure is different—muscle groups and the very enzymes that go through our bodies are all different.

So let's revisit emotions for a second. Women tend to externalize their emotions through tears or displays of frustration, while men in similar situations may channel their emotions into anger. Both responses are valid and reflective of our emotional nature. These differences stem from the unique biochemical makeup of our bodies, with testosterone fueling male responses and progesterone influencing ours. Research indicates that women are more likely to cry than men, with studies showing that women cry an average of thirty to sixty-four times per year, compared to men's average of six to seventeen times.[40] Additionally, the influence of testosterone in men is associated with heightened aggression and increased testosterone levels, corresponding with a greater likelihood of aggressive responses to perceived threats.[41] In contrast, progesterone, which is more prevalent in women, has been linked to nurturing behaviors and emotional bonding, illustrating how these hormonal differences shape emotional expressions.[42] Furthermore, a survey by the American Psychological Association revealed that 30 percent of women feel comfortable expressing emotions openly in comparison to 15 percent of men, highlighting the societal influences alongside these biological factors.[43]

Rather than viewing these differences as limitations, we should embrace them as sources of strength and power. Our distinct emotional expressions offer a valuable perspective and contribute to a more nuanced understanding of the human experience. By recognizing and embracing our inherent differences, we can tap into the full potential of our own unique capabilities.

Let us celebrate the diversity that exists between men and women, understanding that our distinct biochemical compositions shape our responses and emotional expressions. Instead of conforming to societal expectations that may stifle our authentic selves, we should harness the power of our differences and use them to our advantage. By so doing, we are reworking social norms in real time.

ON ANOTHER NOTE

Many women have entered contact sports like boxing and football, which, in the long run, can damage their bodies, especially reproductively. Let me bring some clarity here. I am not saying that we should not participate in contact sports. We have the freedom to do whatever we want. We are free to do those things, but the reasoning behind doing them is often flawed due to our need to compete on a man's level.

When women do those things for the wrong reasons, we reinforce the very traps that bind us. Whether consciously or unconsciously, some of us tend to play into the traps themselves by continually trying to fit in, especially in male-dominated situations. Our efforts to fit in distract us from sharpening our natural skills and using them for the greater good.

UNDERSTANDING FEMALE EMOTIONS

She remembered who she was and the game changed.

—LALAH DELIA

The subject of emotions and the interplay between nature and nurture in shaping societal perceptions of women is a multifaceted and intricate topic. Extensive research has shed light on the existence of inherent biological and psychological distinctions between men and women, which can impact their leadership styles and emotional manifestations. Let's take a closer look at what some experts have found about the way female leaders express their emotions. For instance, a study by J. Smith dives into the unique challenges women face when showing their feelings, often finding that their emotional displays are examined more closely than those of their male colleagues.[44] It's interesting to note that while society tends to expect women to be empathetic, this characteristic can be seen in different lights—some view it as a positive strength, while others might chalk it up to a weakness. In another study, L. Taylor sheds light on how culture plays a significant role in this conversation.[45] In some cultures, women are actually encouraged to express their emotions, which can really boost their leadership skills. On the flip side, in cultures where traditional gender roles are strictly followed, women's ability to show these traits may be suppressed, making it harder for them to navigate their careers and get recognition in male-dominated workplaces.

This overall research highlights the necessity of changing the way we view emotional expression in leadership roles. However, it is also crucial to recognize that the influence of nature and nurture is not mutually exclusive but rather intertwined. While biological factors may lay the foundation for certain emotional tendencies, social and cultural conditioning also play a pivotal role in shaping how emotions are perceived and expressed. Societal expectations, gender norms, and upbringing can shape women's self-perception and their understanding of how emotions should be displayed.

Acknowledging this complexity allows us to challenge and redefine traditional notions of leadership and emotional expression. It empowers us to embrace our innate qualities while also breaking free from restrictive stereotypes.

In essence, understanding the interplay between nature and nurture in the context of emotions and societal impressions of women enables us to navigate the intricacies of leadership with greater awareness and authenticity. It empowers us to embrace the full spectrum of our emotional capacities and utilize them as sources of strength, resilience, and compassion in our personal and professional endeavors. It is also important to note that these differences are not necessarily fixed or innate and can be influenced by socialization and environmental factors. Women may be socialized from a young age to be more nurturing and emotional, while men may be encouraged to suppress their emotions and focus on assertiveness and competition. These socialization processes shape the way women and men express and manage their emotions.

A study conducted by researchers at Harvard Business School explores the complex dynamics of gender and leadership in-depth, offering fascinating insights.[46] The research highlights that women often exhibit higher levels of empathy and emotional intelligence—traits that are proving to be crucial for effective leadership. Interestingly, these natural inclinations are also shaped by societal and cultural influences. From a young age, women are typically encouraged to be nurturing and express their emotions openly, whereas men may be taught to be assertive and emotionally restrained. This combination of nature and nurture provides a richer understanding of leadership and encourages us to question old stereotypes.

By considering these dynamics, the study pushes for a new approach to leadership that celebrates diverse emotional expressions as strengths. This shift not only fosters resilience and compassion but also helps break down limiting stereotypes. Embracing this perspective allows leaders to harness their full range of emotional capabilities, leading with authenticity and empathy. Ultimately, this approach doesn't just make us better leaders; it makes us more self-aware and compassionate individuals.

The discussion surrounding emotions and the interplay of nature and nurture in women's leadership underscores the critical need to identify and challenge gender biases and stereotypes. It calls for the establishment of more equitable and inclusive leadership cultures that embrace a diverse range of leadership styles and emotional expressions.

Women today increasingly recognize the power of emotions and how they can use emotions to their advantage in various aspects of their lives, including in leadership and decision-making roles. They also increasingly recognize the importance of emotional expression and vulnerability in building meaningful connections with others. By sharing their own experiences and emotions, women can build stronger relationships and foster greater empathy and understanding. In the workplace, women are advocating for more inclusive and supportive cultures that value emotional expression and empathy.

Overall, women today are leveraging their emotional intelligence and expressive abilities to create positive change in the workplace.

FACT CHECK

Earlier, I mentioned the differences between the physical makeup of males and females. Let's discuss a few definitive ways that men and women are different. To preface this discussion, I cite Natalie Wolchover's concise definition and explanation of the term regarding differences between male and female makeup. She states the following: "'Sexual dimorphism' is the scientific term for physical differences between males and females of a species. Men and women are more physically similar than different."[47] Nonetheless, a few key distinctions in physiques set men and women apart. Some of them are designed to suit each sex for the role it plays in reproduction, while others exist to help us tell each other apart and aid in our mutual attraction.

Here are some of the cited differences:[48]

- Women have breasts, whereas men have flat chests (but still with nipples on them).
- Men and women both have cartilage surrounding their voice boxes, but because men have bigger boxes (which give them deeper voices), their chunks of cartilage protrude more. This gives them neck lumps called Adam's apples.
- The more testosterone a man has, the stronger his brow, cheekbones, and jawline. Meanwhile, the more estrogen a woman has, the wider her face, fuller her lips, and higher her eyebrows. In short, sex hormones control the divergence of male and female facial features.
- In general, men are more muscular than women. Women are just over half as strong as men in their upper bodies, and about two-thirds as strong in their lower bodies.
- While the male metabolism burns calories faster, the female metabolism tends to convert more food to fat. Women store

the extra fat in their breasts, hips, and buttocks and as sub-
cutaneous fat in the bottom layer of their skin, which gives
women's skin its softer, plumper feel.

- Male and female bodies are well designed for each gender's
role in a primitive society. Women are built for carrying and
birthing children, so they must have wider hips and keep extra
fat in store for the ordeal of pregnancy. Men, free from the
requirements of childbirth, benefit from being as strong and
lithe as possible, both in their search for food, and when in
competition with other men.

So, while it may seem I am stating the obvious, acknowledging
these differences is important to our discussion. Our physiological
makeup, as females, supports our purpose in the species to replicate.
However, we are unique individuals who possess the free will to pursue
any ambition we desire. The point I am trying to make is that we
should not get caught up in the competition to become what we are
not, simply to prove a point, when our innate skills and talents may
lie elsewhere. Recognizing these differences is not about limiting what
we can do, but about understanding our innate strengths and leveraging them to our advantage. This acknowledgment, far from being a
constraint, opens up a world of opportunities for us to boss up in our
own unique, powerful ways.

Just as there are differences between men and women, there are also
unique variations among women. Let me illustrate this with the example
of my sister and me. I, personally, embody a more assertive and competitive nature. When I set my sights on a goal, I wholeheartedly pursue
it, constantly challenging myself to surpass my latest achievements.

My sister, on the other hand, is a natural nurturer. Her love for
children has been a central part of her life, as she has dedicated herself

to raising and caring for them. With seven children of her own, her nurturing abilities have become a perfected art. It's really fascinating to think about how my sister and I turned out so different, even though we grew up in the same household. We both learned similar values and had shared experiences, but our unique personalities have taken us in different directions. My sister has this wonderful nurturing ability that makes her shine in caregiving and connecting with others, while I've leaned into being more assertive and independent in what I do. It's a great reminder that even within the same family, each of us can forge our own paths and evolve based on our individual traits and experiences. By celebrating what makes us different, we not only enrich our own lives but also add to the incredible diversity of perspectives in our family and wider community. My sister and I embrace and celebrate our innate qualities. We harness and refine our individual talents to create fulfilling lives for ourselves and our families. As a collective group, women should adopt the same mindset: accepting and embracing their unique gifts and leveraging them to build the best lives they can.

THE SOCIAL MEDIA ALGORITHM OF LIFE: THE BOURDIEUSIAN FRAMEWORK

Social conditioning is real. Believe it or not, it lives and breathes daily in the lives of women and men. Society imparts certain influences on us and then expects us to respond to those influences in a certain way.

The Bourdieusian framework illustrates this. It relates to the dynamics of power in society, especially the diverse and subtle ways that power is transferred and social order is maintained within and across generations.

I call the Bourdieusian framework *the social media algorithm of life*. Even though it was published decades ago, it still aptly describes the set of rules society determines for us. It highlights how we interact in society. Think about what social media does for us. It allows us to share ideas and information, and by doing so, we influence each other.

This framework studies the differential treatment of girls and boys in traditional Western society, which promotes gender-biased attitudes in how girls are raised. In essence, this framework speaks of the intergenerational disparities in a social setting, specifically the acquisition of two very important embodiments of cultural capital. The concept of intergenerational disparities highlights the profound impact that societal norms and expectations have on the upbringing of boys and girls, influencing their future opportunities and roles. Within traditional Western society, gender-biased attitudes often dictate the treatment of children, nurturing distinct skill sets and characteristics that can limit their potential. This framework underscores how these biases perpetuate a cycle where girls may not be encouraged to aspire to leadership roles, affecting their ability to acquire essential cultural capital. As we progress through life, the interpersonal dynamics shaped by our upbringing influence how we perceive and attain our goals, particularly in positions of authority. It speaks to how we gain capital as we grow to become who or what we are trying to be, especially in leadership roles.

There are two distinct concepts I would like to address. First, here is *cultural capital*, which includes deeply ingrained habits, skills, and dispositions that we possess due to our life experiences. Second, the Bourdieusian framework introduces the concept of *habitus* as a form of cultural capital, whereby societal influences shape our experiences and establish long-lasting ways of believing and living. Essentially, cultural capital shapes the skills and habits we develop, influencing how we think, feel, and behave in our everyday lives. So habitus is basically how our ways of thinking and behaving are influenced by the society we grow up in. It shapes how we see things and how we act throughout our lives. The premise is that our habits are ingrained in us from birth and perhaps even in the womb before birth.[49]

The Bourdieusian framework highlights the concept of capital, which extends beyond material possessions to include social capital. Cultural capital plays a crucial role in shaping our societal roles and influences the power we hold within a given culture. However, it is important to recognize that men are often socially conditioned from an early age to possess greater social capital and leadership abilities, while we as women may face additional challenges in accumulating and asserting our own cultural capital.

I REMEMBER WHEN ...

I recall a time growing up when we all sat at the table as a family for dinner. As with most of our dining interactions, several social norms were at play. I can still see in my mind's eye sheer beige curtains blowing slightly in the wind over the window in the dining room. As my dad spoke, most times the girls didn't say much, just a giggle and an occasional head nod. The boys on the other hand were very vocal, even the brothers younger than me. They were encouraged to speak boldly and voice their opinions. The girls were often "shushed" if we said too much, so we mostly stayed quiet.

After dinner one particular night, I recall getting up from the table and scraping my plate into the trash then pulling the bag out to take the trash outside, and my mom said, "Oh no, let the boys do that. Come in the kitchen and help me and your sisters with the dishes." My brothers were building social capital while the girls stood down and behaved as expected. During this time in history, social behavioral norms for boys and girls were playing out in households across America. There was no thought of these behaviors being anything but normal.

POINT OF REFLECTION

How did my kitchen table story make you feel? I realize that my story lacks twenty-first-century appeal, but it is reflective of societal norms still greatly present today. Many of you reading this book are descendants of this very same social conditioning passed down from previous generations. Now, imagine how different you think today and how differently you feel about raising girls. These feelings and expectations are no accident. They are part of the evolution that we are experiencing and prove that the inevitability of changes in social norms is unstoppable!

MOVING FORWARD

In this chapter we explored the various societal constraints and expectations that women face, which often stifle their potential and limit their opportunities for growth and success. This chapter highlighted the subconscious effects of societal norms that can keep women from reaching their full potential. We discussed how these "traps" manifest in the form of gender biases, stereotypes, and cultural conditioning that influence women's choices and opportunities.

In the next chapter, I will discuss the concept of the Glass Cliff, which refers to the precarious positions women often find themselves in when they reach leadership roles. The goal is to connect theoretical insights with everyday experiences to provide a deeper understanding of the challenges to diversity and inclusion women continue to face.

CHAPTER 4

The Glass Cliff

A Slippery Slope

I do not wish women to have power over men, but over themselves.
—MARY WOLLSTONECRAFT

I am an African American female in the financial services industry. Throughout my career, I have found myself in positions where I was not expected to succeed. One situation that I remember vividly was during one of many financial advisor summits in Scottsdale, Arizona. As one of the few women in the group and the only African American woman at the time, I was not expected to survive for the next event. White men dominate the financial services industry. It is a difficult field for women to succeed in because investors, especially from the baby boomer generation, mostly trust white men to handle their money. At the summit, I overheard a group of men taking bets that I would not be around for the next summit and paying each other off for lost bets that I would make it to the current one. They laughed and said, "She is doomed. No one with any real money will work with her." Even the wonderful white man who appointed me to the organization sincerely wanted me to succeed but, quite frankly, did not think that I would be successful either.

That was in 2005. Today, in 2024, I am one of the few top African American female advisors in the industry, relatively speaking. In 2024, African American women continue to be significantly underrepresented in the financial advisory field. According to the Bureau of Labor Statistics, only about 6.4 percent of personal financial advisors are Black, and of that, an even smaller percentage are women.[50] This underscores the rarity and achievement of being a top African American female advisor in the industry today. I accept the challenge of being silently doubted and use it as my fuel to excel. I do not let the banter of doubters alter my course.

Although I persevered, I was not oblivious to others' lack of confidence in my professional and leadership abilities. I knew doubt circulated in the air, but I did not understand the underlying forces fueling that doubt. I am not sure if a specific term had been coined at that time. Through my studies, I began to understand how the Glass Cliff correlates with events that happened in my professional career as well as how countless other women experience the Glass Cliff phenomenon.

A SLIPPERY SLOPE

We have all heard of the glass ceiling, that seemingly impenetrable barrier that keeps some of us women from advancing in our careers. Many times, we look up with optimism, seeing only opportunity before us. But it is only a mirage of opportunity. The Glass Ceiling is hidden in plain sight. Merriam-Webster defines "Glass Ceiling" as "an intangible barrier within a hierarchy that prevents women or minorities from obtaining upper-level positions."[51]

The term Glass Ceiling and its meaning are well known and understood. However, as women continuously break through the glass ceiling, there is a stealthier challenge waiting on the other side.

The Glass Ceiling warrants attention as we connect it with the Glass Cliff and how the two are set to operate in unison, one after the other. Women who successfully penetrate the Glass Ceiling are met with another challenge: they must work to get a firm grip that will help them avoid sliding off the Glass Cliff.

CORNERSTONE OF THE GLASS CLIFF

Glass Cliff Theory illuminates the precarious position that modern women face in asserting their leadership power within a male-dominated society. In this chapter, I delve into numerous examples to unveil its undeniable aim. By gaining a deeper understanding of this theory, you will be empowered to actively effect change.

The Glass Cliff is a concept that highlights the precarious positions women often find themselves in when appointed to leadership roles. Coined by researchers Dr. Michelle Ryan and Professor Alex Haslam, the theory suggests that women are more likely to be appointed to top jobs during times of crisis or downturn, when the risk of criticism and failure is highest.

Grace Back describes the Glass Cliff as a situation where women are more frequently appointed to high-stakes positions, such as CEO or prime minister, during periods of instability.[52] Kathy Caprino notes that women are given leadership roles under circumstances that differ significantly from those of men, often involving increased risk and potential failure.[53] This reflects a broader pattern of gender discrimination, where women are placed in challenging positions that may be less stable and harder to succeed in.

Yael Oelbaum adds that the Glass Cliff effect is a subtle yet significant form of gender discrimination that hinders workplace diversity and limits women's success in leadership roles.[54] She notes that women are often preferred for these precarious positions as a means for organizations to signal change.

Susanna Whawell highlights that, while women may reach high-level positions, they are disproportionately represented in unstable roles.[55] This phenomenon is not limited to specific industries or regions but is a widespread issue where women are tasked with solving nearly insurmountable problems. When these efforts fail, the responsibility is placed on the women, leading to their resignation or dismissal, which perpetuates the stereotype that women are unsuitable for leadership.

These perspectives collectively underscore the heart of the Glass Cliff: women are often set up to fail in senior positions, reinforcing existing norms and systems that challenge diversity and inclusion in leadership.

Theories like the Glass Ceiling and the Glass Cliff emerge from observed patterns in society, indicating that they are, to a significant extent, influenced by prevailing social norms. When researchers identify a pervasive bias against female leaders, they formulate theories to explain these social dynamics. In turn, these theories provide an academic framework that helps society understand and, ideally, challenge the status quo. Thus, it can be argued that social norms initially inform the development of theories, which subsequently reinforce, critique, or attempt to alter these norms. This dynamic interaction means that theories and social norms are mutually influential, with societal behaviors and academic insights continually shaping each other in an evolving dialogue.

The Glass Cliff aids in the examination of the interaction between societal perceptions and organizational factors that undermine women's successful attainment and tenure in the upper echelons of management and leadership positions across the board. The theory explains the way in which those in control (usually men) allow a minority of woman to ascend to a leadership position where the risk of failure is extremely high. The ideas behind Glass Cliff Theory add to the dimension of male majority rule by delving into how men control women's upward mobility.

DEEP DIVE

The problem with Glass Cliff appointments relates to the presumption of expendability. Researchers and scholars maintain that women are put in high-risk positions to be used as scapegoats and shoulder the blame if things go terribly wrong. Glass Cliff appointments are one of many barriers to upward mobility and sustainability for women in leadership positions and can be affirmed from multiple well-documented resources. Nonetheless, unethical recruitment practices that increase the chances for women to advance to Glass Cliff appointments require continued research. The advancement of women to leadership positions shows significant strides over the last century. There are more female CEOs, judges, senators, business owners, and world leaders than ever before in the history of the world.

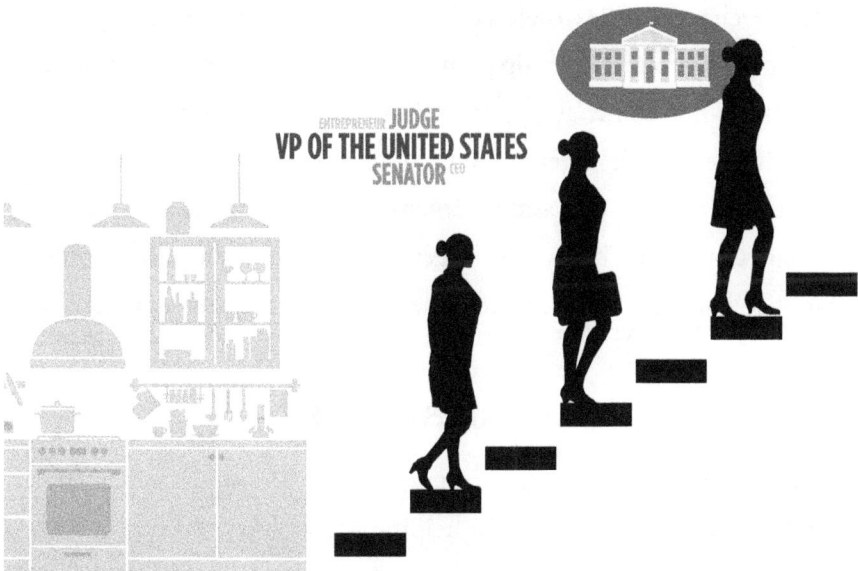

ENTREPRENEUR JUDGE
VP OF THE UNITED STATES
SENATOR CEO

Despite optimistic growth in female representation, leadership positions continue to be male dominated. A scan across Fortune 500 companies and government positions reflects that women remain underrepresented. A respondent from the Ryan, Haslam, and Postmes study testing the Glass Cliff phenomenon had this to say:

> I think the Glass Cliff is another form of the glass ceiling, intended to block women's passage up the ranks. Women will be put in Glass Cliff positions because there is a resentment of ambitious women who are often seen as threatening or difficult (not just by men) and also because it gives those who appoint them the excuse that they do allow women (superficially) equal opportunities and therefore allows them to avoid any charge of sexism.[56]

Essentially, the Glass Cliff is a facade. Its deception gives false hope to aspiring female leaders. Women exert unrelenting energy to climb the leadership ladder. They wait with desperate patience just for the chance to flex their skill sets and demonstrate quality leadership. However, leadership chances rooted in Glass Cliff appointments do not count as opportunities anticipated by those waiting with immeasurable potential. Glass Cliff opportunities truthfully set out to misuse and toss aside women's time and talents and preserve a male-dominated culture of leadership. It is as if the value women work so hard to build and strengthen is deliberately set as a sacrifice.

BY THE NUMBERS

Kathy Caprino is a renowned career and leadership coach, author, and speaker who specializes in helping professional women achieve success and fulfillment in their work. In an effort to explain obstacles that executive-level leaders face and ways they can avoid them, Caprino stated:

> The most compelling piece of data that surprised me was that women are more likely to be promoted to the top—whether it's CEO or at any C-suite level—when the company is facing a downturn or a crisis. That's when boards are more open to appointing someone other than the traditional white, male CEO. And among CEOs leaving office over the past 10 years, a higher share of women has been forced out than men (38% of women vs. 27% of men), because when a company isn't recovering from a crisis, it's often the people at the top who get axed. Look at some of the female CEOs today, and it's easy to spot the so-called "Glass Cliff" hires. Marissa Mayer at Yahoo, Meg Whitman at Hewlett Packard, Mary Barra at General Motors, Irene Rosenfeld at Mondelez (formerly Kraft)—all these women were appointed to the top job in order to turn their respective companies around. To date, all these women have kept their lucrative jobs, but other female CEOs haven't been so lucky. For example, former Yahoo CEO Carol Bartz; former head of Merrill Lynch Smith Barney, Sallie Krawcheck; former co-President of Morgan Stanley, Zoe Cruz, and former Avon CEO, Andrea Jung—these are just some of the women who essentially fell off the Glass Cliff.[57]

Taking a closer look at a few of the female CEOs mentioned in Caprino's statement illustrates the circumstances in which they were appointed. Denise Morrison of Campbell Soup Company, Phebe Novakovic with General Dynamics, Meg Whitman at Hewlett Packard, Mary Barra at General Motors (GM), and Irene Rosenfeld at Mondelēz International (formerly Kraft)—all these women were appointed to the most visible position in their organizations during sex scandals, huge operating losses, accounting scandals, and major reconstruction. As forward thinkers, each of them likely had researched and analyzed the entire situation before taking it on, so they knew what they were getting into. These women accepted risky appointments expecting to turn their respective companies around at precarious times. While Glass Cliff assignments are risky, and failure may derail careers, these women fearlessly accepted the challenge.

To date, many of these women continue to hold these prestigious positions, but others (such as the individuals Caprino mentions) have not been so lucky. They were either dismissed or resigned. As Kathy Caprino puts it, these women essentially "fell off the Glass Cliff." As of January 1, 2023, there are only fifty-three female CEOs of Fortune 500 companies.[58]

Looking at numbers only gives us a piece of the picture. Numbers do not lie. They are hard facts. They paint a clear picture of the under-representation of women in executive leadership roles.

However, they are incapable of showing us soft data, such as what outstanding women leaders say, how they handle themselves in challenging situations, and exactly what makes them worthy of executive leadership appointments.

LEADING BY EXAMPLE

Let's consider Phebe Novakovic, who was appointed as CEO of General Dynamics in 2013 at a time when the company was suffering a $2 billion loss in the previous quarter. Novakovic continues to lead General Dynamics, and the company is better off as a result. During a *Washington Post* interview, she was asked, "Did you think a woman could become the CEO of a defense company?" She answered:

> So, I have always worked in the national security environment, which was heavily male. I never really thought about the difference between men and women in the workplace, although we are different. So, I didn't really think about the maleness of the organization. What attracted me to General Dynamics is that it was different. I'm not an engineer. I have not risen through the ranks from 25-years old. I've had a fairly … unusual background. And the CEO and chairman at the time was a trial attorney from Chicago.
>
> And I thought, oh, there's a bit of an iconoclastic culture here. And maybe there's a place for me. You know, so much in life is about finding your place, whether it's with your family, in your community, your nation, and in your company. And there was a place for me.[59]

Phebe Novakovic epitomizes the fearlessness and fortitude necessary to not only stand as a female leader during a difficult time but to also lead with valor and competence.

Another example is Meg Whitman. She was appointed to the CEO position at Hewlett Packard during a time of slow growth. The previous CEO, a male, stepped down. I imagine that there was a lot of tension in the company when she was put in charge. The announcement of her appointment to the position included a short speech by her predecessor, Raymond Lane. During the announcement, Lane stated:

> We are fortunate to have someone of Meg Whitman's caliber and experience step up to lead. We are at a critical moment, and we need renewed leadership to successfully implement our strategy and take advantage of the market opportunities ahead. Meg is a technology visionary with a proven track record of execution. She is a strong communicator who is customer focused with deep leadership capabilities.[60]

These women, like so many other capable, competent, and fearless leaders, consciously make the choice to accept risky appointments. And despite the Glass Cliff appointments, they thrive!

On the other hand, some women are deprived of opportunities to lead because of their perceived competence and capacity to lead. This was the case during the 2016 presidential election, during which formidable candidate Hillary Clinton experienced an unexplainable loss. In 2008, former president Barack Obama stepped onto a slope just as slippery as the Glass Cliff. Both Obama and Clinton experienced situations closely related to the Glass Cliff as they attained or attempted to attain an executive leadership position in our country. We will explore the circumstances surrounding their situations.

NAVIGATING THE PRECARIOUS EDGE: BARACK OBAMA'S HIGH-STAKES PRESIDENCY

Catherine J. Taylor of Cornell University coined the term *occupational minority* to refer to a worker who is a numerical rarity in his or her occupation, such as men who are nurses or women who are engineers.[61] This concept differs from the notion of being a *token*, which is typically defined at the workplace level.[62] By contrast, occupational minorities exist at the national level.[63] That being said, occupational minorities are women or minority individuals who are typically denied the privilege of certain positions or occupations.

The "white savior effect," a cousin of the Glass Cliff, refers to the deliberate positioning of a white man after a woman or an occupational minority has "fallen off the cliff." This strategic positioning makes the white man appear to have saved the day. Basically, white male leaders are projected in Western society to perform more successfully than occupational minorities. The white savior effect works to promote the notion that women and minorities are not suitable to hold certain positions. The situation fosters distrust and diminishes expectations of women and minorities for high-level leadership roles.

Fast-forward to the 2008 election of President Barack Obama. There is no better example of the Glass Cliff–white savior phenomenon in modern times than this election. Though he was elected by the will of the people as the first African American president, we all know that the Electoral College ultimately decides who holds that office.

Scholars studying the Glass Cliff and related concepts have discussed the challenges faced by President Obama, suggesting that he was expected to fail upon taking office during a tumultuous period in American history. This aligns with Glass Cliff Theory, which posits that minorities are often placed in leadership roles during crises when the likelihood of failure is high.[64] Elected in the aftermath of the 2008 financial crisis, President Obama was thrust into a leadership role amid unprecedented economic turmoil, with banks and financial institutions embroiled in scandals.[65]

The narrative around Obama's presidency suggests that his election was influenced by the belief that occupational minorities possess qualities beneficial in times of crisis, such as calmness and nurturing.[66] This aligns with the idea that he was seen as uniquely equipped to address social challenges, a sentiment often associated with minority leaders placed on the "Glass Cliff."[67] Despite successfully navigating the country through the crisis, Obama faced portrayals of failure, underscoring the persistent scrutiny minority leaders endure.

Following President Obama's tenure, the 2016 presidential election saw the emergence of Donald Trump, an unexpected nominee whose victory can be interpreted through the lens of the "white savior" effect. This concept suggests a return to traditional leadership archetypes following a minority leader, reinforcing the notion of white male superiority in leadership roles.[68] The election overshadowed the credentials of Hillary Clinton, who faced gender-based biases that further illustrated systemic obstacles for women in leadership.[69]

The portrayal of President Obama during his presidency was marked by significant scrutiny, with some narratives attempting to undermine his accomplishments and frame him negatively. This aligns with the "white savior" effect, a concept where the achievements of minority leaders are downplayed to set the stage for a subsequent white leader to be seen as a rescuer. The election of Donald Trump can be viewed through this lens, where the shift back to a white male president was perceived by some as a return to traditional leadership. Despite Trump's unexpected candidacy, the broader political context suggests a desire for continuity in traditional leadership archetypes. This underscores persistent societal biases that favor white male leadership while challenging the capabilities of minority leaders. The theory suggests that after President Obama was supposed to fail miserably, the white savior (a white man) was to come behind him and save the day. This is how we ended up with President Donald Trump as president. No one expected Donald Trump to be the nominee, not even Donald Trump himself. However, a white man had to assume the role of president after President Obama in order for the white savior effect to take place. The next president, the white savior, had to be a white man, no exception. In this context, Hillary did not stand a chance.

Many political analysts argued that Obama's election was an example of the Glass Cliff phenomenon, as he was appointed to lead the country during a time of great uncertainty and risk. Obama's election was also seen as a reaction to the failures of the previous administration, which had been dominated by white male leaders.

While Obama's election was a historic moment for the country, it also highlighted the challenges that women and minorities face when appointed to leadership positions. Obama's presidency was marked by intense criticism and opposition, with many questioning his legitimacy as a leader and his ability to navigate the complex political landscape.

Despite these challenges, Obama was able to enact significant policy changes during his presidency, including the passage of the Affordable Care Act and the legalization of same-sex marriage. His success in office serves as an example of how individuals can overcome the Glass Cliff and thrive in leadership positions, even in the face of significant obstacles.

HILLARY CLINTON DENIED
THE CLIFF EXPERIENCE

Women are the largest untapped reservoir of talent in the world.
—HILLARY CLINTON

Hillary Clinton is an occupational minority because she is a woman. Following the Glass Cliff–white savior logic, Clinton's presidential bid launched during a political climate in which she could not be allowed to win. The country's transition from Obama's presidency (one that garnered unjustifiable criticism) to new leadership made for an unsettling political climate. Had we been in a state where the economy and the country were status quo, she probably would have been elected. Because the white savior had to be a white man, though, she could not succeed President Obama.

Clinton was in the right place at the wrong time. As a former first lady of the United States, US senator, and secretary of state, Hillary Clinton had already shattered many levels of the Glass Ceiling.

There is no doubt she would have demonstrated competence as a president. But due to the Glass Cliff–white savior mechanisms at play, she could not win. That is why she won by votes but was not named president. She won but did not win. She was denied the opportunity to even stand on the cliff. Herein lies yet another example of the cross of challenges that women bear. Challenges are nothing new. In fact, anyone seeking or currently traveling the leadership path should expect them, especially women.

Are the Glass Ceiling and Glass Cliff situations real? Yes. Are they a part of obstacles that women leaders face? Without a doubt. Do those obstacles form challenges that we must encounter and navigate? Absolutely! Despite the accepted perception of doubt and statistics that show the underrepresentation of women in executive leadership positions, many of our untold stories are ones in which we continue to break Glass Ceilings and make firm, progressive steps of success without falling off of the Glass Cliff.

COMING TO GRIPS WITH THE GLASS CLIFF PHENOMENON

The Glass Cliff, the white savior, and occupational minorities all reflect societal perspectives on women and minorities in leadership. These ideas represent the unspoken nature of gender bias—classic examples of how male majority rule controls the consciousness of organizational behavior across all facets of leadership.

As women, we should expect challenges in our career paths because we deal with such things as male majority rule, double binds, gender bias, and a host of other obstacles that exist to interrupt our ascension to leadership. The Glass Cliff is one of the more calculated interruptions. Understanding the premise behind Glass Cliff Theory sheds light on the interaction between societal perceptions and social positioning.

MY GLASS CLIFF PERSPECTIVE: EMBRACING CHALLENGES, OWNING SUCCESS

Situations characterized by a looming Glass Ceiling or the treacherous Glass Cliff present formidable challenges for women leaders. However, it is crucial for us to be outspoken and assertive, regardless of the obstacles we may face. This entails speaking up during the selection process, making it clear that we are fully aware of the existing circumstances and expressing our well-thought-out plans to navigate the turbulent terrain with unwavering confidence.

Consider this hypothetical example: a female executive is appointed as CEO of a struggling tech start-up following the departure of a male leader. This company has faced significant financial issues, and morale among employees is low. Despite these obstacles often linked to the Glass Cliff phenomenon, the new CEO approaches her role with clarity and purpose. She begins by conducting thorough research on the company's challenges and developing a strategic turnaround plan that includes open communication with her team and clear performance metrics.

Recognizing the unique difficulties she faces, she schedules one-on-one meetings with team members to acknowledge their concerns while actively involving them in the problem-solving process. During

these discussions, she articulates her vision for recovery, thereby instilling confidence and encouraging collaboration. By leveraging her skills
in crisis management and demonstrating decisiveness, she not only
navigates the turbulent situation but also showcases her leadership
capabilities. This proactive stance allows her to transform potential
failures into opportunities for success, ultimately leading the company
toward a more profitable and stable future. Through this example,
we see how women leaders can own their narratives surrounding the
Glass Cliff, focusing on strategic agency and resilience rather than
merely the obstacles presented to them.

MODERN-DAY CLIFF EXPERIENCES

In recent years, several prominent examples of the Glass Cliff have
emerged, highlighting the unique challenges faced by women in leadership roles.

The resignation of Kimberly Cheatle as CIA director exemplifies
the harsh realities faced by women in leadership roles, particularly
during periods of political instability. Despite her extensive experience
and dedication to national security, Cheatle became an unfortunate
scapegoat amid the swirling controversies surrounding intelligence
operations and the broader implications of the Glass Cliff phenomenon. It is crucial to recognize that her resignation was not a reflection
of her competence or actions, especially as she had no direct involve-
ment in the issues that led to the uproar. Instead, Cheatle's departure
highlights the challenging dynamics at play, where female leaders
are often unjustly held accountable for crises beyond their control,
illustrating the persistent gender biases that can hinder their professional legacy and contributions. Following her resignation, Cheatle
was replaced by a male counterpart, which not only perpetuated the

narrative of male authority during crises but also reinforced the notion of the white savior complex. His appointment came with promises to restore stability and regain public trust, signaling a missed opportunity to acknowledge and elevate the contributions of women leaders like Cheatle, who have often navigated these tumultuous waters with resilience and skill. This sequence of events reflects how leadership transitions can inadvertently reinforce systemic biases while sidelining the diverse perspectives necessary for comprehensive solutions to complex national issues.

Another notable instance involves Gina Haspel, who became the first female director of the CIA in 2018. Haspel's appointment came during a turbulent period following various controversies surrounding the agency, placing her in a high-pressure situation where she had to navigate public scrutiny while rebuilding trust within the organization.

Similarly, Blanca Duran, who took on a leadership position at CenterPoint Energy, faced significant obstacles when she was appointed during a time of restructuring and increased regulatory challenges for the utility company. As the first woman to hold this executive role, Duran was tasked with not only managing existing crises but also implementing innovative strategies for sustainable growth amid skepticism from stakeholders.

Amy Palcic, a former vice president of communications for the Houston Texans football team, encountered her own Glass Cliff scenario when she took charge during a highly contentious election cycle. Her role was fraught with challenges, including public backlash and internal disagreements, as she sought to enhance the party's image and communicate effectively with a divided audience.

Former White House press secretary Jennifer Psaki resigned amid a cascading wave of controversy, citing the need for a fresh approach to foreign policy in a climate rife with distrust and division. Following

Psaki's resignation, her position as White House press secretary was filled by her deputy, Karine Jean-Pierre, a move that drew attention to the prevalent white savior complex often observed in political transitions.

This phenomenon, where predominantly white leaders are positioned as the solution to issues faced by marginalized communities, raises questions about the underlying motivations for such appointments. Richard Grenell's candidacy, for example, was framed within a narrative that suggested a need for a strong, assertive figure to restore order and credibility to US foreign policy, despite the potential erasure of the contributions made by women and leaders of color.

The trajectory of leadership transitions within the intelligence community and political sphere underscores a troubling pattern where accomplished women, including Gina Haspel, Blanca Duran, Amy Palcic, and Kimberly Cheatle, have been replaced by white men, reinforcing the archetype of the "white savior." This recurring theme not only diminishes the visibility and contributions of these women in pivotal roles but also perpetuates the systemic biases that favor male leadership, particularly during challenging times.

Still Bossing Up

One modern-day example of a woman who succeeded despite facing the Glass Cliff phenomenon is Mary Barra, the CEO of GM.

Barra was appointed as CEO of GM in 2014, shortly after the company had emerged from bankruptcy and was facing numerous challenges, including recalls of millions of vehicles due to faulty ignition switches. Barra was the first woman to lead a major global automaker, and her appointment was seen as a sign that GM was committed to changing its culture and becoming more inclusive.

Despite the challenges facing GM, Barra has been widely credited with leading the company through a period of significant transformation and growth. Under her leadership, GM has focused on investing in electric and autonomous vehicles, expanding into new markets, and improving its operations and efficiency.

Barra's success at GM is a testament to her leadership skills, her ability to navigate challenging circumstances, and her commitment to creating a more inclusive and equitable workplace culture. Her appointment as CEO of GM also serves as an inspiration for other women who may face the Glass Cliff phenomenon, showing that it is possible to succeed in leadership positions even in the most challenging of circumstances.

MOVING FORWARD

Now that we have thoroughly discussed the odds against our journey to lead with courage and competence, it is time to shift the conversation. We will look at the catalyst and forward thinker, the shero.

In the next chapter, I will define "shero" through a psychological analysis, examine how she is today's strong woman, and explore how to raise sheroes, build career capital in our girls from birth, and address threats to the shero's progress. This next discussion will add depth and richness to the description of the current rise of the great nation of shero women.

CHAPTER 5

A Shero Defined

A woman is the full circle. Within her is the power
to create, nurture, and transform.
—DIANE MARIECHILD

In this chapter, we dive into the concept of a shero and what it means to be one. A **shero** is a term used to describe a woman who exhibits extraordinary bravery, leadership, and resilience, often in the face of adversity and societal challenges. Sheroes are not only found in prominent positions of power or fame but also in the everyday lives of ordinary women who perform remarkable acts of kindness, sacrifice, and strength. These women, whether recognized or not, play pivotal roles in shaping communities and supporting those in need.

Merriam-Webster defines a "shero" as "a woman regarded as a hero."[70] On the other hand, Urban Dictionary defines a shero as "a woman or man who supports women's rights and respects women's issues."[71] I define a shero as an evolved woman who stands in her own truth, even when it is difficult. She rises to any occasion, changing what she can change, accepting what she cannot, and passing the lessons learned to women coming behind her. She expects more from the next generation than the last.

The evolution of a Shero Nation is the heroic movement of women who embrace change and use it to empower women so that we no longer expend energy trying to compete with men but instead use that energy to challenge ourselves. In doing so, we create a world that accepts us as we are and respects and recognizes our true and natural strength.

THE BOLD AND THE SILENT: TWO FACES OF THE SHERO SPIRIT

Bold sheroes are often those who hold visible leadership roles—trailblazing executives, passionate activists, or influential public figures like Kathy Caprino who champion the causes of gender equality and professional success for women. These women serve as beacons of inspiration and courage, using their platforms to drive significant social change and empower others.

Equally important are the **silent sheroes** who operate away from the limelight. Grandmothers who step in to raise their grandchildren, providing them with stability, love, and guidance; volunteer women who dedicate countless hours to feeding the homeless, ensuring no one in their community goes hungry; and everyday heroes who offer support to friends, family, and strangers alike without seeking recognition. These silent sheroes embody the spirit of compassion and community, making substantial impacts through their unwavering dedication and selflessness.

Together, both bold and silent sheroes contribute to the tapestry of society, exemplifying the strength and grace of women across all walks of life. Their stories, whether widely told or quietly lived, deserve to be celebrated and honored for the profound difference they make in our world.

As we explore the psychological profile of a shero, we find that she possesses a unique blend of qualities that make her a charismatic champion, collaborative team player, fearless leader, and much more. From the past to the present, sheroes like Susan B. Anthony and Hillary Clinton have left their mark in their respective fields by embodying at least ten of these characteristics. Understanding the essence of a shero is crucial to empowering future generations of women and fostering a Shero Nation that values and respects women's true and natural strength. The top twenty-five characteristics of a shero, which I will detail later in this chapter, provide a set of guiding principles that young women can use to cultivate the mindset, habits, and behaviors that will enable them to be more mindful of their goals and their propensity to achieve them.

The information presented in this chapter is vital to millennial sheroes for several reasons. First, it provides a clear definition of what it means to be a shero and helps young women understand their potential and the qualities they naturally possess to become effective leaders. By identifying the characteristics of a shero, millennial women can evaluate their own strengths and weaknesses and work on building powerful social capital.

Second, this chapter addresses some of the challenges that millennial women face in their pursuit of power. I speak to the threat of objectification buy-in and how it can undermine the progress of the shero movement. By raising awareness of these issues, this chapter encourages millennial sheroes to stay vigilant and to actively work toward creating a world that respects and recognizes the true strength and potential of women.

Finally, the information presented in this chapter addresses the debate around narcissism and its prevalence among the younger generation. It highlights the potential double-edged nature of narcissistic traits, which can either yield productive and powerful results or lead to unproductivity and a misuse of time. This is particularly important for millennial sheroes, who are often criticized for their level of self-regard and have been labeled the "narcissistic generation." By understanding how to channel narcissistic tendencies, millennial sheroes can better prepare themselves for the challenges of the world and be more purpose driven.

It is important to note that not all millennials possess narcissistic traits, and research provides no definite correlation between the millennial generation and the personality trait of narcissism. Nonetheless, the discussion around narcissism and its potential effects is a valuable tool for millennial sheroes to reflect on their own behavior and make deliberate and intentional behavioral choices.

To the bold and unapologetic women who proudly embrace the terminology of "The Unstoppable Shero," I commend you for owning your power and refusing to let anyone diminish it.

Some may criticize the term "shero" as being too cutesy or minimizing the struggles that women have faced throughout history. However, we must remember that we own the right to define ourselves, our movements, our struggles, and our triumphs. We cannot let outside influences interrupt our thought process and make us doubt the validity of our own experiences and accomplishments. Sheroes we are!

As women, we have the right to create and embrace language that reflects our empowerment and celebrates our achievements. Just as men have coined terms and phrases to describe their accomplishments and movements, we have the right to do the same without apology.

We must continue to stand in our power, speak our truth, and embrace our identity as sheroes. By doing so, we not only honor the struggles of the women who came before us but also pave the way for future generations of empowered women. So embrace your inner shero and let your voice be heard.

KNOWING THE SHERO

Knowing the essence of a shero gives insight into her potential and suggests ways to help her capitalize on opportunities. Truthfully, I had to go through this reflective process to understand myself as well as my fellow sheroes.

With a better understanding of who we are as sheroes, I welcome you into discussions about raising sheroes and how to prepare future shero generations to carry the torch for the continued forward progress of women and their right to female expression without judgment. Together, we will also explore threats to the shero evolution, particularly how millennial women are changing the dynamics of sexism and consequently creating what I call the "objectification buy-in." The objectification buy-in is a concept that requires me to explain the full thought process behind my observation and its adverse effects. The objectification buy-in, its influence on young sheroes, and the shero perspective on the discussion will be presented later in the chapter.

First, let us get a clear understanding of what shero means.

PSYCHOLOGICAL PROFILE OF A SHERO

The shero's feminine and "super" human qualities enable her to courageously fight for justice and freedom, often in the face of formidable odds and personal harm or danger. After researching and conducting numerous interviews with modern-day sheroes, I noted the following traits:

Trait	Description
Attentive, active listener	Great at practicing active listening and staying present in conversations
Charismatic champion for a cause	Has a magnetic personality and is passionate about making a difference
Collaborative team player	Values teamwork and is great at working with others toward a common goal
Confident	Believes in themselves and their abilities
Courageous	Willing to take risks and face challenges head-on
Discerning follower	Has the ability to follow and take direction while still thinking critically and making their own decisions
Decisive	Good at making quick and confident decisions
Encouraging	Lifts others up and motivates them to reach their full potential
Fearless leader	Has the ability to lead with courage and conviction
Insightful exhorter	Offers wise and valuable advice to others
Inspirational	Has the ability to inspire and uplift others with her words and actions
Lifelong learner	Always seeking out new knowledge and experiences
Mission driven	Focused on achieving their goals and making a positive impact
Optimistic	Has a positive outlook on life and sees the best in others
Passionate	Driven by their passions and interests
Patient mentor	Willing to take the time to guide and mentor others

Trait	Description
Proactive	Takes initiative and is always looking for ways to improve
Purpose focused	Aligns their actions with their values and purpose
Resilient	Able to bounce back from setbacks and challenges
Respectable character attributes	Values integrity, honesty, and respect for themselves and others
Spiritual	Nurtures their spiritual well-being and connection to something greater than themselves
Stylish	Has a great sense of personal style and is always on trend
Supportive	Offers unwavering support to friends, family, and colleagues
Willing role model	Sets a positive example for others to follow
Wired for victory and success	Has a mindset that is focused on achieving success and winning in life

A shero, celebrated or silent, possesses at least ten of these traits, significantly influencing her sphere of work and life—empowering every shero, bold and silent, to make lasting impressions across homes, communities, cities, states, and nations, propelling forward the cause of women globally.

POINT OF REFLECTION

Reflecting on the stories of both bold and silent sheroes, it's valuable to consider: **Which of these qualities do you see in yourself? Which do you recognize in some of your own personal sheroes?** Everyone has the potential to embody the strength, compassion, and resilience that these women demonstrate, whether through visible acts of leadership or silent gestures of support. Take a moment to identify and celebrate the qualities within you and those you admire that contribute to making a positive impact on the lives around you.

RAISING A SHERO

The modern-day woman raises a shero by what I call deliberate parenting. I recall raising my children almost on autopilot. I was protective and engaged in their lives. But for the most part, I followed the social road map of that day for raising children. My parenting was very attentive and conscious. I protected and nurtured my children by making sure they were fed, keeping them safe, and positioning the right influences around them.

On the other hand, what I call deliberate parenting is consciously teaching our children, both boys and girls, how to build social capital. In short, social capital boils down to visibility. Your confidence, poise, and sense of self attract attention. Your very presence in the arena you revolve in reflects your level of social capital. In business, a high degree of social capital contributes to your success, allowing you to build a sense of shared values and mutual respect. Boys tend to build higher degrees of this social capital than girls through socialized male versus female activities growing up.

Boys, then, must be taught that girls exist as powerful godly creations with their own feminine strengths and abilities—not to be judged but to be respected and appreciated. This ingrained respect will not interfere with how boys build social capital but will complement the building of social capital in girls. Our girls must be taught lessons to reach beyond what society imposes, without trying so hard that they lose the feminine gifts that God gave them. Those gifts are powerful as well.

Young sheroes must be taught in such a way that feeds their conception, which will shape and guide their growth. Self-reckoning and the ability to stand firm and speak your mind among your peers will help build social capital. This should be taught from birth. Young sheroes will begin building social capital by being awakened to how and when social capital is built. This capital is formed partially from a process of deliberate, formal teaching and learning, but is primarily generated through immersion in the sociocultural environment present in the early family and schooling.[72] Childhood years are the most important in the formation of habitus and capital.[73] Through observing and listening to those around them, children internalize appropriate ways of behaving and interpreting the world around them, thus acquiring the capital associated with their habitus.[74]

Deliberate parenting can result in the development of sheroes. One person I recognize as a deliberate parent is Richard Williams, the father of Venus and Serena Williams.[75] Mr. Williams deliberately parented his girls. He went to the heart of what his daughters would face with their entrance into the tennis world. He utilized intentional language to make them strong and enable them to take what was going to come against them, including all the racial discrimination. He raised them in such a way that they remain strong, articulate, and able to stand in their own truth. They wore their braids with their hearts on their sleeves. They took punches and, in most instances, have remained graceful and articulate. They stand strong in the face of blatant discrimination. That was deliberate parenting.

I imagine him saying to his daughters, "This is what you're going to face, but I want you to stand strong and take what this world's going to dish out to you and still rise." Those are two sisters who were raised as sheroes. Through deliberate parenting, the Williams family helped Venus and Serena build not only social capital but also life skills that helped them weather the storms of bias and prejudice that they are certain to continue encountering while carrying the torch of leadership in the world of tennis.

POINT OF REFLECTION

If you are a parent, how do you describe being a deliberate parent? After reading this content, do you feel that you may change your parenting approach? Consider how the concept of deliberate parenting can influence your own practices and how it might help you raise confident, resilient, and socially conscious individuals, both boys and girls, who can navigate the complexities of our modern world with grace and strength. As a parent, being deliberate means actively choosing to consciously and intentionally raise your children in a way that prepares them for the challenges they may face in life. It involves being aware of societal norms and biases and deliberately countering them with positive reinforcement and empowering messages.

After reading about Mr. Williams's deliberate parenting style, perhaps you have been inspired to adjust your own parenting approach. Deliberate parenting is not about sheltering your children from adversity, but rather equipping them with the tools and mindset to handle it confidently. By instilling values of self-worth, resilience, and social consciousness in our children, we can raise them to be strong and confident individuals who are able to stand up against discrimination and injustice.

ABOUT MILLENNIALS

Like each generation, millennials move, act, and behave in their own unique way. Without a doubt, millennials are making their imprint on society by changing societal norms, which supports the rise of the Shero Nation.

Millennials differ from previous generations. In their Pew Research article, Kristen Bialik and Richard Fry comment on key distinctions between millennials and other generations:

> Now that the youngest millennials are adults, how do they compare with those who were their age in the generations that came before them? In general, they're better educated—a factor tied to employment and financial well-being—but there is a sharp divide between the economic fortunes of those who have a college education and those who don't.
>
> Millennials have brought more racial and ethnic diversity to American society. And millennial women, like Generation X women, are more likely to partici-pate in the nation's workforce than prior generations.

Compared with previous generations, millennials—those ages 22 to 37 in 2018—are delaying or foregoing marriage and have been somewhat slower in forming their own households. They are also more likely to be living at home with their parents, and for longer stretches.

And millennials are now the second-largest generation in the U.S. electorate (after Baby Boomers), a fact that continues to shape the country's politics given their Democratic leanings when compared with older generations.[76]

Instead of moving out and establishing their own households, millennials take advantage of educational pursuits and opt to stay home longer. They prioritize self-establishment, self-improvement, and self-gratification over assuming traditional independence.

Their self-absorption alarms outsiders who liken their behavior to narcissism. For those concerned about the course of our society, this is of particular concern, especially since millennials are a relatively large population, which means their focus and decisions will greatly impact societal norms.

THREATS TO THE SHERO'S EVOLUTION

The way we talk to our children becomes their inner voice.

—PEGGY O'MARA

In today's fast-paced world, the millennial generation faces the unique challenge of balancing self-awareness with societal expectations. As they navigate their formative years, millennials often encounter the risk of becoming overly self-focused, a trend that has sparked debates around narcissistic traits within this generation. This focus on the self can serve as a double-edged sword: it can empower individuals to become confident and purpose-driven sheroes or lead them to unproductivity and self-absorption. The most significant threat lies in misdirecting this self-focus, resulting in a lack of purpose and the potential for the objectification buy-in, ultimately hindering personal and societal growth.

The millennial generation faces a significant challenge when it comes to balancing self-focus with societal expectations. In an era where self-regard is often criticized as narcissism, the time millennials spend investing in themselves can either lead to empowerment or unproductivity. The decision to focus inward can foster personal growth and resilience or, if misdirected, can result in wasted potential. For millennial sheroes, this delicate balance of purpose versus self-absorption represents both an opportunity for development and a threat to their future success. Without a clear sense of direction, the very traits that could enable them to thrive may instead undermine their ability to make meaningful contributions to society.

BALANCING SELF-FOCUS AND PURPOSE

Currently, there is an academic debate about millennial trends and narcissism. The Mayo Clinic describes the personality disorder of narcissism as "a mental condition in which people have an inflated sense of their own importance, a deep need for excessive attention and admiration, troubled relationships, and a lack of empathy for others."[77] Current research continues to explore narcissism and its prevalence in the younger generation. The scientific debate regarding millennial ties to narcissism continues. Some researchers claim that millennials possess greater narcissistic traits, whereas other researchers cite findings that refute those claims.[78]

In reality, all individuals possess certain narcissistic traits. Extensive research has not established a definitive connection between the millennial generation and the clinical diagnosis of narcissistic personality disorder. Therefore, in this discussion, we will explore these traits and examine how harnessing them can yield a dual outcome, one of either empowerment or unproductivity.

Take our generation of millennial sheroes, who avail themselves of extended time of living in their parents' home, for example. The question becomes whether or not they truly capitalize on this valuable option. How do they spend extra time at home that might otherwise go toward working to build a life with a significant other or raising children? Will their type of self-absorption later benefit them? The answer is "possibly." This very question plays into Social Role Theory, as it almost expects certain behaviors to play out—further evidence of the power of societal norms and expectations.

Sheroes who use extended time in their parents' home as an interval or season to deeply know themselves, reflect on life occurrences, and engage in emotional and financial preparation will likely leave their parents' home purpose driven and better equipped to face challenges of the real world. They are more apt to take on and "push through the massive transformations that society periodically undertakes."[79] In this case, focusing on "self" yields powerful and productive results.

On the other hand, sheroes whose time at home is solely invested in the external will likely yield opposite results. Purpose must be prioritized. Otherwise, focus without purpose will result in unproductivity, a misuse of fleeting time. Researcher Michael Maccoby validates this: "Narcissism can turn unproductive when lacking self-knowledge and restraining anchors. Narcissists become unrealistic dreamers."[80]

Society criticizes millennials for their level of self-regard and has labeled them the "narcissistic generation."[81] Whether or not they are a narcissistic generation, millennials are definitely more attuned to themselves and their needs,[82] which can be a double-edged sword. The appropriate focus on self can serve as a catalyst for the development and preparation of sheroes. On the other hand, a misdirected focus can threaten the development of potential sheroes while robbing them of time and energy. Moreover, it can lead them to an even greater threat of objectification buy-in.

THE OBJECTIFICATION BUY-IN

I define objectification buy-in as *the tendency to buy into and perpetuate objectification of women*. The constant barrage of sexually suggestive images in media and social media has led to an "objectification buy-in," where women voluntarily contribute to their own objectification.

This behavior is particularly harmful to millennial women who grew up with technology and unfiltered access to information. While social media allows women to express themselves and their differences, it also promotes objectification, setting back progress made in changing attitudes toward women. By buying into objectification, women are contributing to societal impressions that women are unsuitable for leadership, should not be taken seriously, and are only suitable for visual entertainment. This buy-in creates an obstacle to progress and slows down the evolution toward more positive and meaningful social perceptions of women. Ladies, beware!

The negative effects of this phenomenon on social expectations for women cannot be understated. It perpetuates a superficial standard, reducing women to mere objects of visual appeal rather than recognizing their intelligence, capabilities, and contributions. This objectification infiltrates every aspect of life, from professional settings to personal relationships, reinforcing detrimental stereotypes that limit opportunities and undermine confidence. Young girls observing this culture are indoctrinated with the belief that their worth is inherently tied to physical appearance and sexual appeal, leading to skewed priorities and diminished self-esteem. The consequences of objectification buy-in are far-reaching, not only stifling the individuals who succumb to it but also halting societal advancement toward gender equality. It is imperative to challenge and dismantle these harmful norms, promoting a culture where women are valued for their genuine abilities and strengths, not just their physical allure.

THE LAW

Despite the persistent challenges we confront on the path to achieving gender equality, one of the most pressing battles we continue to fight revolves around our reproductive rights. Despite the assurance that the law should safeguard and uphold these rights, we find ourselves in a ceaseless struggle for autonomy over our bodies and reproductive choices. As we grapple with wage gaps and other gender-based disparities, it is disheartening to witness legislation falling short of addressing these pressing issues, particularly when it's often conceived and approved by a male-dominated legislature, further perpetuating the inequality we endure.

In the face of these daunting obstacles imposed by an unbalanced legal system, we stand firm and resolute. Surprisingly, the lack of robust legal support has only steeled our determination, igniting a fierce resolve within us. We are rapidly advancing toward a tipping point where we will wield the power to reshape laws and become a majority voice in enacting legislation that directly influences our lives. We are on the cusp of seizing the power to reshape the very laws that have hindered us, emerging as a predominant voice that will craft legislation directly impacting our lives.

To seize this power, we are taking the following specific actions:

1. **Political mobilization:** We are actively working to increase women's representation in government by supporting and promoting female candidates. Through fundraising, campaign support, and voter mobilization efforts, we aim to elect officials who prioritize gender equality and women's rights.

2. **Advocacy and lobbying:** We engage in rigorous advocacy efforts to influence lawmakers' decisions. We lobby for the introduction and passage of legislation that address gender-related disparities, reproductive rights, and other critical issues affecting women.

3. **Legal challenges:** We pursue legal challenges against discriminatory laws and policies. These challenges are meticulously planned, supported by legal experts, and aimed at setting legal precedents that protect and advance women's rights.

4. **Public awareness campaigns:** We continue to raise awareness about gender inequality and the importance of legal reform. Through social media, public events, and educational campaigns, we keep the spotlight on these issues and encourage public support.

5. **Media engagement:** We engage with media outlets to tell our stories and share our message. By working with journalists and using various media platforms, we ensure that our issues gain wide visibility.

6. **Policy development:** We collaborate with policy experts and legal scholars to develop comprehensive proposals for legislative reform. These proposals serve as the foundation for the laws we aim to create or amend.

With unwavering determination and a comprehensive approach, we are actively working toward our goal of reshaping the legal landscape to better protect and advance women's rights. Our collective efforts are propelling us forward, and we are steadily approaching the day when we will have significant influence over the laws that govern our lives.

But there is more work to be done.

THE SHERO PERSPECTIVE

This chapter covers a lot of ground, including the definition of a shero, the challenges and threats that sheroes face, and the complex issues of narcissism and objectification. It can be overwhelming to think about how future generations can embrace their inner shero given all of these factors. However, I believe that collective action is key.

By standing together, supporting one another, and using our political and legal systems to defend our freedoms, we will continue to make progress. It is also important to educate ourselves about the obstacles that sheroes face, including the perpetuation of social expectations and theories that limit and threaten our growth. With this knowledge, we can work toward enacting laws that support sheroes and empower young people to shift attitudes and challenge societal norms. Ultimately, it is up to us to equip the next generation with the mindset and tools they need to make a difference.

The solution to objectification buy-in is simple. Stop looking to the external world for validation of beauty. We are all beautiful, divinely favored, and perfectly imperfect. This is not to imply that external beauty is not important, because God also gave us our very own sense of vanity. The key is to join the two forces—your internal strengths and your external beauty—creating a force to be reckoned with! We will talk about some of the more well-known women who have done just that in chapter 6. But remember, we all have the same abilities as these women to find and tap into our own greatness!

THE DOMESTIC LANDSCAPE OF THE MILLENNIAL WOMEN

When it comes to gender roles and the way women are perceived, millennials are making significant strides in a positive direction. Women in this generation challenge traditional norms and expectations and are more educated than their male counterparts. This is particularly evident in the changing views toward women's roles in domestic settings.

Millennials possess the potential to drive the most transformative changes in the evolution of sheroes over the next two decades.[83] With their boldness, uninhibited nature, drive, and technological proficiency, they hold the key to shaping the future. It is crucial that we collectively come together to support and educate these millennial sheroes, ensuring that the influence of objectification does not hinder their progress or trigger a detrimental paradigm shift in our evolutionary journey.

BRINGING IT ALL TOGETHER

Women embody resilience in all aspects of life, from thinking to developing, building, nurturing, and restoring. As sheroes, we cannot be defined by a single definition, as our nature is constantly evolving. Some women may not have yet realized their shero nature, but we all have a responsibility to explore our greatness beyond societal norms and limitations imposed by a male-dominated society or our own beliefs. Some may not even be aware of the barriers that hinder their progress, such as the unproductive aspects of narcissism, the harmful effects of objectification, or age-old societal norms. Therefore, we need support and education from others during this critical stage of development. The shero movement must proactively prioritize mentorship for girls and young women, nurturing them into catalysts of positive change for the advancement of women, particularly in leadership roles. It is our responsibility to seize this opportunity, a vision pursued by the sheroes who came before us.

MOVING FORWARD

In this chapter, we discussed a range of topics related to women and leadership, including the definition of a shero, the challenges and threats that sheroes face, and the importance of building social capital for girls. We also touched on issues such as objectification, narcissism, and traditional gender roles, and how these factors can impact women in society.

Throughout, we delved into the remarkable capacity of women to embody resilience as thinkers, creators, builders, nurturers, and healers. The shero movement bears a crucial responsibility in guiding and empowering young women as catalysts for transformative change.

Undoubtedly, the battle for gender equality persists, particularly concerning the need for greater representation of women in leadership positions. Yet, armed with heightened awareness and a deeper comprehension of the obstacles and possibilities that lie ahead, we can forge ahead. There is still much work to be done, but our collective efforts will continue to propel us closer to our shared vision.

THE *unstoppable*
SHE

stoppable
HERO ♀

THE *unstop*

CHAPTER 6

From Shadows to Spotlight

The Evolution of Women's Role in Society

Feminism is not about making women stronger. Women are already strong. It's about changing the way the world perceives that strength.

—G. D. ANDERSON

Understanding the journey of women's rights and suffrage is crucial to fully appreciating the struggle, achievements, and perseverance that have paved the way to where we stand today. This historical perspective sheds light on the immense efforts and sacrifices made by countless women who dared to challenge the status quo and fight for equality. It is through this lens that we can grasp the true essence of the word "evolution" in the context of women's rights—a continuous, incremental progression fueled by unwavering determination and courage.

The evolution of women's rights is marked by pivotal moments and relentless advocacy. From the historic Seneca Falls Convention of 1848, where the seeds of the suffrage movement were sown, to the tireless work of suffragists like Susan B. Anthony and Elizabeth Cady Stanton, and the eventual ratification of the 19th Amendment in

1920, every step forward has been a testament to the resilience and fortitude of women. These milestones were not mere events; they were profound shifts that gradually transformed societal norms and expanded the realm of possibilities for women.

However, the journey did not end with the right to vote. The fight for true equality continued, intersecting with other critical movements such as civil rights, and extending into modern times as women strive for representation and leadership in all facets of society. This ongoing evolution underscores the importance of knowing and understanding our history. By reflecting on the past, we honor the legacy of those who fought before us and gain inspiration to continue pushing forward. Looking back at how it all started is a step that cannot be skipped.

WHERE IT ALL STARTED

The 1848 Seneca Falls Convention is widely recognized as the catalyst for the women's suffrage movement in the United States. It was the first women's rights convention, where activists like Elizabeth Cady Stanton and Lucretia Mott gathered to advocate for women's rights, including the right to vote. The Declaration of Sentiments, modeled after the Declaration of Independence, was presented, demanding equal rights for women, marking the beginning of organized efforts for women's suffrage.[84] During the twentieth century, leadership of the suffrage movement passed through two organizations, the National American Woman Suffrage Association (NAWSA) and the National Woman's Party (NWP). Due to the joint efforts of the NAWSA and the NWP, the 19th Amendment was finally ratified in 1920. This is the most substantial achievement of women in the Progressive Era.

Historians describe several waves of feminism in history: the first in the nineteenth century, growing out of the antislavery movement, and the second in the 1960s and 1970s.

MOMENTOUS TIME IN HISTORY

The Seneca Falls Convention of 1848 was the first event dedicated to advocating for women's right to vote. Calling it historic is an understatement—it was momentous and paramount. This gathering showcased the courage and determination of women in the 1800s, who, despite being oppressed by societal circumstances, stood firm with unwavering conviction.

Despite potentially paralyzing forces surrounding them, the sheroes of Seneca Falls pressed on. Their planning, presentation, and subsequent follow-through on the declaration set forth at this convention illustrated the courage and fortitude of women that had not been realized, acknowledged, or respected. As a precedent to other landmark events that would follow, this convention laid the groundwork for incremental strides in women's rights.

Frederick Douglass was the only African American present at the Seneca Falls Convention, while no Black women were among the hundreds of attendees discussing women's rights. History shows that it would take another seventy years for women's suffrage to be secured by the US Constitution through the 19th Amendment. However, while this amendment marked a significant milestone for many women, it was not until decades later, with the passage of the Voting Rights Act, that women of color were fully able to exercise their right to vote. The 19th Amendment played a pivotal role in propelling the women's suffrage movement forward, igniting the evolution of the "shero" spirit.

THE PIVOTAL MOMENT IN HISTORY

Approximately one hundred years ago, a pivotal moment in American history took place: Congress passed the 19th Amendment granting women the right to vote in 1920. This marked a great victory for trailblazing sheroes of the past and those standing in patient and optimistic wait. This was certainly a turning of women's empowerment tides. It was a pivotal turning point because it unbridled the voice of women and allowed each one of us more control of our lives.

Women gradually progressed from spectators to active participants. They went from being heard as voices muffled by restraint and resistance to speaking with amplified voices expressing the need for more change. The change was slow but progressive. It encapsulates the twentieth century as a whole—a time of unprecedented change and unparalleled movement forward caused by the fearless, tireless efforts of our shero predecessors.

Historically speaking, the evolution of sheroes can probably be traced to a time before slavery. However, the second Anti-Slavery Convention of American Women in 1838 serves as a glimpse of this evolution. Mary Grew of Philadelphia, an abolitionist, formed the group in an effort to coordinate the work of female antislavery societies.

At this convention, Black and white women met to hear prominent abolitionists speak, while outside, men and boys threw rocks at the building in protest of Black and white women meeting together. Prior to the meeting, the mayor made it clear that the meeting should be held and attended by white women only. The women refused; they joined hands, formed a human chain, and stood united against the crowd of men who tried to stop them. The next day, the mob burned down the building where these women met while police and firefighters stood and watched.[85] The mob was exonerated of all charges. Racism was part of the women's suffrage movement from the outset. This is yet one more

110

incremental stride of the women's movement in the nineteenth century and a show of unity in the common fight to be heard.

Decades later, women of color were given the right to vote through the Voting Rights Act of 1965. The 19th Amendment continued building momentum for the women's suffrage movement, and events such as the first Anti-Slavery Convention, held on May 9–12, 1837, were also contributing factors to its success.

THE TWENTY-FIRST CENTURY

Enter the twenty-first century, where women have taken charge of their education and emerged as the most highly educated group in the nation. We now occupy esteemed positions such as top political offices, judgeships, and seats in the US Senate throughout the country.

This remarkable movement has persisted for a significant duration, with men historically resisting its progress at every turn. As the prevailing powers, they strive to maintain their dominance until the bitter end. However, their efforts are in vain, as the unstoppable evolution of sheroes marches forward. Women are entitled to more than mere survival; we have the right to attain our rightful place in society. From advocating for equitable minimum wages to triumphing in multimillion-dollar sex discrimination lawsuits, we, as women, have persistently fought and will continue to fight for true equality.

WOMEN IN ACTION: SHAPING JUSTICE, ACTIVISM, AND LEADERSHIP

One isn't necessarily born with courage, but one is born with potential. Without courage, we cannot practice any other virtue with consistency. We can't be kind, true, merciful, generous, or honest.

—MAYA ANGELOU

On January 21, 2017, the world witnessed the largest protest in US history: the Women's March. Millions of women across the United States, alongside allies from sixty other countries, took to the streets in an unprecedented demonstration of unity and strength. This protest embraced the full spectrum of American women, representing diverse backgrounds, ethnicities, and identities. Participants carried signs and chanted slogans, voicing their demands for equality, justice, and respect. The goal was to stand in solidarity and fight for women's rights, emphasizing issues such as reproductive freedom, equal pay, healthcare access, and protection from gender-based violence. The Women's March became a powerful catalyst for change, igniting a global movement that continues to advocate for the rights and dignity of women everywhere.

There has been a consistent, silent building of the tidal wave in the process of reshaping the face of this nation's leadership. 2019 was an exceptional year for a group of women in Harris County, Texas, where nineteen African American women were elected judges. This is especially unusual because Houston, though one of the most culturally diverse cities in the nation, has often not reflected that in its justice system leadership. That all changed as a result of straight-ticket voting.

The women who are currently in judgeships in Harris County include Judge Shannon Baldwin, Judge Lucia Bates, Judge Ronnisha

Bowman, Judge Sharon M. Burney, Judge Dedra Davis, Judge Linda Marie Dunson, Judge Toria J. Finch, Judge Ramona Franklin, Judge Lori Chambers Gray, Judge Angela Graves-Harrington, Judge Cassandra Y. Holleman, Judge Erica Hughes, Judge Maria T. Jackson, Judge Tonya Jones, Judge Latosha Lewis Payne, Judge Michelle Moore, Judge Sandra Peake, Judge Germaine Tanner, and Judge LaShawn A. Williams.[86]

History has proven that empowered women will fight to change unfair situations that plague and hinder their forward motion. Studies suggest that female leaders have a behavioral repertoire that includes more communal features than their male counterparts.[87] As a result, women receive disapproving and uncooperative reactions more often than men when they act in an assertive or direct manner.[88]

However, women-centered leadership also has positive effects in times of crisis. This was evident in the midst of the COVID-19 pandemic. Here we address the difference in results (number of cases and deaths) and the handling of the pandemic between female-led nations versus male-led nations during COVID-19 and the striking revelation that was a main point of discussion in 2020.

Crisis is a true litmus test for leaders, both men and women. The pandemic tried and tested the great leaders of the world like no other twenty-first-century malady. Stereotypical female qualities based on innate emotional sensitivity and physiological differences may give men pause, but women are also known to have stronger interpersonal skills and a collaborative leadership style. There are inherent qualities that come with the authentic feminine mystique. Research shows, "Countries with women in leadership suffered six times fewer confirmed deaths from COVID-19 than countries with governments led by men. Unsurprisingly, the media swelled with stories of their pragmatism, prowess—and humanity."[89] Female leaders in places like New Zealand, Taiwan, and Iceland have all been applauded for their effective strategies in combating the virus.[90] Their success has led to wider conversations regarding male versus female leadership styles.

The pandemic brought visibility to the strong, powerful, and efficient wiring of women and their effective management of crisis situations. In fact, their leadership strength and skillful crisis management abilities are coming to the forefront in the face of nations around the world. The progress of women cannot be denied. The title of Garner's article (2020) poses a poignant question: "Female Leadership During COVID-19: What Can We Learn?"[91] Experts argue that any leader can be successful if he or she is able to demonstrate a balance of strength and compassion. For women, strength and compassion are natural talents.

Shelley Zalis, founder of The Female Quotient and a leading advocate for workplace equality, offers a powerful conclusion to this discussion:

> Perhaps COVID-19 has shown the world what should have been obvious all along: The qualities that make women excellent caregivers are also what make them great leaders.[92]

THE YOUNG SHERO'S FUEL

As an African American child back in the day, I recall living much of my childhood in gray scale—nothing spectacular about it, nothing particularly devastating either—until one of the most pivotal moments occurred. My father died suddenly from a heart attack at the age of forty-two. I was only twelve years old. Mind you, I grew up during a time where the man was the provider, and the woman stayed home and raised the children. When he died, I felt lost. My relationship with my dad was very special, as I was his first from my mom's second marriage. Being dark skinned and bony with very short hair during the sixties made for a vicious time. But my dad always made me feel special. He always told me that I was smart and beautiful, and one day I would show the world just how special I am.

My dad was a very controlling man. What he said was gospel in his house. My dad was naturally talented. I guess he had to be. As the eldest of nine siblings all born in a small shack in Quitman, Mississippi, he was forced to drop out of school in the sixth grade to help care for and provide for his younger siblings. He had to be strong; he had to be the authoritarian figure of eight younger siblings, which I imagine was not easy at all. So my father was no nonsense! But he had a soft heart for his children, and he taught me so much through his strength. He constantly expressed very high expectations of me as his first born, much like his dad had for him. And although I was smack-dab in the middle—I have three younger siblings, one who has gone on to be with the Lord, and three older siblings—I was strong willed and determined to make something of myself.

I remember exactly how my dad made me feel as if it were yesterday. My dad worked for the Santa Fe railroad as a porter, but he always wanted more for himself and for his family. He was in the process of opening Green's Auto Parts when he died. I remember him taking me with him to work at the shop at night after he got home from work. He was in the process of building the shelving and wiring of the building. Although never formally trained, my father was very skilled with electricity, thank God. I remember he wired our garage to ring the doorbell so that we could not sneak into the house at night and come in through the garage door. My older sisters and brothers caught heck trying to do that! I watched him intently. I learned from him intuitively. I soaked up his fuel and grew strong internally but was afraid to show it. As a young girl during that time, I was expected to behave like a lady. I played the piano and learned to bow and curtsy.

AN UNCONSCIOUS SHERO

With the family breadwinner gone, we all felt lost as a family. My mom, skittish and jumpy, crumbled at his death. She worried how she would care for seven children ranging from eighteen to two years of age. When I turned thirteen, my mom had to find work to supplement her widow's benefit. Back then, many Black women were housekeepers. So she took odd jobs cleaning houses for white families in the all-white community of La Cañada, California. I watched her come home every day after undoubtedly long hours of back-breaking work to feed and take care of all of us. It just tore me up inside.

One day she took me to work with her, as she often did. As I sat in the kitchen, I noticed that she got very quiet. I looked and called for her in that big, beautiful house with no answer. I found her sitting in a chair asleep. I gazed at her resting face. She was exhausted. At that very moment, I said to her, "That's it. You are not doing this anymore!" She first looked at me as if to say, "Girl, please." But something in her made her listen to me.

She looked into my little thirteen-year-old face and said, "But I don't know how to do anything else."

"We will figure it out," I reassured her. The next day, we bought a newspaper and looked through the want ads (that's what they were called back then). I spotted a position as a microfilmer at the Broadway Warehouse. The position required that she sit and feed receipts through a film machine that created microfiche. I helped her complete the application. I went with her to the interview, sat in the lobby, and waited. She interviewed and got the job. She worked for that warehouse for many years until the warehouse closed. She then went on to find work with the Bank of America card center in Pasadena where she worked for twenty-plus years and retired.

All this occurred while I was growing up. I graduated high school, went to college, and began taking care of myself. By this time, I walked with strength and independence but still unconsciously operated within the expected social guidelines for a woman. As I entered corporate America, I was subjected to prejudice, favoritism, gender bias, and discrimination. I took the opportunities I could get at the time, all of which were "gender appropriate" positions. This was the norm for someone who worked hard for advancement, so I did not challenge the opportunities or circumstances. I unknowingly walked amid a fog of unconsciousness.

Later, I married and had children. My then-husband and I sent our children to private schools all of their young lives. I was adamant that they speak articulately and use their words to express their feelings. For some reason, that was very important to me for them. I worked long hours, and my aunt took care of them after school. But one day, after coming home from working hard all day, my daughter asked me, "What we gon' eat?" At that moment, I paused and considered all the money that I was paying to educate my kids. When she asked me that question in that way, I told myself that I had to be present to raise my own kids. So I left corporate America and opened a large daycare facility near our home. That way, I was able to take my children to school, pick them up, and bring them straight home every day. I was in control over the influences in their lives. I successfully ran the largest daycare in Altadena, California, until the very month that my son graduated from high school. Afterward, I sold the daycare and started my private financial practice. Reflecting on my journey, I realize that understanding and acknowledging my history has been vital. It has allowed me to appreciate the strength I have gathered along the way. This perspective reinforces the idea that knowing where we come from is essential to comprehending our present and valuing the resilience that shapes us.

MOVING FORWARD

As the saying goes, "If you don't know your history, then you are doomed to repeat it." This wisdom underscores the necessity of historical awareness. Looking back at how we arrived at our present state is not just an academic exercise but a vital step in ensuring we do not lose sight of the hard-won gains and the ongoing struggles. It is through this reflection that we recognize the patterns, the progress, and the setbacks, equipping ourselves with the knowledge to forge a better future.

In essence, the story of women's suffrage and rights is a powerful reminder of the enduring spirit of evolution—an ever-advancing journey shaped by the collective efforts of those who came before us. Understanding this history is not optional; it is a crucial step that cannot be skipped if we are to continue the legacy of progress and equality.

CHAPTER 7

Asunder

The Unbreakable Shero Nation

The future belongs to those who believe in the beauty of their dreams.
—ELEANOR ROOSEVELT

In a world where barriers still persist and inequities continue to challenge us, a formidable force emerges—an unbreakable coalition of sheroes, united and undeterred. This chapter delves into the resilient spirit and relentless drive of women who refuse to be divided or diminished.

THE EVOLUTION OF A SHERO: FROM SUPPRESSION TO SELF-ACTUALIZATION

I was born into a world where Black people were oppressed and often misguided. My early childhood was shaped by the basic societal constructs for African American families, where the limiting belief that the life of a Black person would not amount to much was prevalent. This idea was ingrained in my environment, and I found a semblance of contentment in it because everyone around me shared these same expectations. It was a comfortable, if constrained, existence.

Then along came bussing. We were suddenly transported to schools far outside our neighborhoods, where we encountered people who did not look like us. Many of us became painfully insecure, surrounded by white people who looked down on us and teachers who held low expectations for us. School became a place that fed our insecurities about our appearances and reinforced the belief that Black girls would end up as teenage moms and Black boys would end up either in jail, on drugs, or dead. Soon afterward, drugs began flooding our neighborhoods, fulfilling these grim predictions for many—dropout teen moms, and our men filling prisons and graveyards.

In my late teens, however, a fire sprang up in me that just would not die. The more society tried to discourage me and hold me back, the more I pushed forward with unrelenting strength and determination. The harder the fight, the stronger I became. By my early twenties, my expectations for my life had changed drastically. I set high goals for myself, visualizing the end result even when the process seemed insurmountable.

At the time I didn't realize it, but I was practicing self-actualization. Self-actualization, as defined by Maslow's hierarchy of needs, is "the realization or fulfillment of one's potentialities, especially considered as a drive or need present in everyone." Maslow describes it as "the highest level of psychological development, where the actualization of one's fullest personal potential is achieved, which occurs only after basic and psychological needs have been fulfilled."[93]

The Shero evolution reflects the ongoing journey toward self-actualization, where women have had to first secure their basic needs—safety, security, and a place in society—before they could fully realize their potential. The rise of the Shero Nation is a testament to this evolutionary path. Women have moved from being subjugated by circumstance to becoming leaders, innovators, and trailblazers in various fields. This progress has been driven by an unwavering commitment to overcoming obstacles and achieving personal and collective goals.

The rise of the Shero Nation mirrors the path of self-actualization. Just as my journey to strength came later in life, the emergence of the Shero Nation is on its own evolutionary path. This makes perfect sense. Before we can reach the most visible place in the shero evolution, we must go through various life events and recognize the undercurrent of the divine that places us where our basic mental needs are met. This evolutionary path is not just a societal shift but a personal one, deeply connected to the struggles and triumphs of the suffrage movement and other challenges women faced in the nineteenth and twentieth centuries.

Women have long faced immense challenges, from the Seneca Falls Convention of 1848, where the first gathering specifically addressed women's right to vote, to the broader suffrage movement and beyond. These historical struggles are not just events of the past; they are the foundation upon which the Shero Nation stands today. The evolution of women's rights and their fight for equality has been a journey marked by both progress and setbacks, illustrating that evolution works regardless of whether the journey is easy or hard.

Recognizing my history has been vital in understanding my present and appreciating the strength I have gathered along the way. The rise of the Shero Nation, much like my personal journey, is a testament to the power of resilience and self-actualization. As we continue to evolve, we honor the struggles of the past and embrace the challenges of the present, knowing that each step, no matter how difficult, is part of our collective growth.

SELF-CARE BREAK

The inevitable rise of a Shero Nation is an evolutionary buildup of situations, activities, and social perceptual shifts all lining up and forcing a change in the patterns, behaviors, and attitudes in society. As we continue to fight for equality, each generation realizes successes that we pay forward to the next generation.

As sheroes we stand in our truth. We own our femininity. We harness our feminine power in ways that motivate and influence people, leaving those around us with no choice but to acknowledge and respect our presence. This rise in power is evolutionary as opposed to revolutionary, and it is happening as we speak.

The powerful evolution of women to their place in positions of power owes its origin to historical battles including enslavement and deliberate attacks against our self-esteem including physical abuse. As our sisters of the past fought and endured these situations, they grew stronger and more determined. Countless strides were made, but much under the strict "supervision" of men.

With divine favor, we became stronger, more educated, and gained the respectful attention of men, yet we continue to face social stigmas and gender bias. Forging through, we began to use education as a catapult into higher echelons of power in the corporate and political worlds. The support of our sisters, increased independence through the accumulation of wealth, some male support, and legal changes helped widen the lanes, allowing more and more of us to come into our own.

Forward movement over previous years foreshadows a greater movement, one that will transform the landscape for women. This chapter describes additional forces including the great wealth transfer, education, community, and other supportive entities behind the shero evolution and what makes it truly unstoppable! The churning evolution precedes the rise of the Shero Nation. This nation confronts adversity and proclaims that nothing and no one will separate it from its emergence and final establishment. Nothing and no one can or will stop this movement.

ASUNDER

The word "asunder" signifies the act of breaking into parts or becoming disunited. In this chapter, I delve into the resilience of the shero evolution, emphasizing its imperviousness to outside interference. However, we must also address internal and external threats that can impede our progress, which cannot be overlooked. The word "asunder" is used to embody the menacing and hostile forces that have historically challenged women's evolutionary strides and efforts.

Picture "asunder" as a relentless adversary, a formidable force whose sole purpose is to tear apart and fracture. A relentless force, unyielding in its determination to disrupt unity and sow discord.

Imagine "asunder" as a shadow that loomed large when women were once reduced to property, subject to the dominion of husbands or fathers. Its bitter presence manifested when men vehemently opposed the 1838 unification efforts of Black and white women, resorting to hurling rocks at their gathering place and ultimately setting the building ablaze.

Nevertheless, we must emphasize that "asunder" did not prevail in the past, and it shall not stage a comeback now. It stands diminished in the face of our ascending nation, dwarfed by its stature.

Our collective strength and unwavering determination have weathered the storms of adversity, and we continue to forge ahead, resolute in our mission to mend the divisions "asunder" seeks to sow.

"Let no man put asunder what God has joined together." This biblical principle underscores the divine favor that drives the evolution of the Shero Nation. Whether one believes in God or not, some things can only be explained by the divine. Our unity, resilience, and strength are gifts from a higher power, and despite the relentless adversary that seeks to divide and destroy, we stand firm. Just as God's will is unbreakable, so, too, is our collective resolve to overcome the challenges of the past and present. We are bound by a higher purpose, and no force can tear apart what is divinely ordained.

THE INEVITABLE RISE

There is no force more powerful than a woman determined to rise.

—W. E. B. DU BOIS

The rise of our great Shero Nation can be likened to the evolution of technology. It is planned and rooted in a need for advancement. Once it arrives, there is no changing it. There is no going back.

The evolution of the Shero Nation is the coming together of women and their innate power as nurturers and leaders. This powerful movement is imminent and as definite as the scripture that declares "what God has joined together, let no man put asunder." It is important to acknowledge that the intent of the phrase "let no man put asunder" is not being used to place blame or cast criticisms on any gender. Rather, it serves as a timeless reminder of the sanctity of human relationships and the commitment to preserving the bonds that connect us. In this spirit, it emphasizes the importance of unity and understanding within the broader context of humankind.

I assert that God's master plan strategically placed each progressive step of the movement. I further assert that God's divine hand moves to aid in this rise. Anytime I reference *asunder* or the inevitability of the movement, I acknowledge the power of divine intervention as the undercurrent supporting all things relevant to the progress of the shero evolution and rise of the nation. I invite you to think through explanations in this chapter about the power behind the shero evolution and how these powers are in motion and cannot be stopped. I discuss wealth, community, and even raw feminine power.

WHAT FUELS THE RISE

As we stand on the cusp of a transformative era, two pivotal forces are converging to reshape the landscape of power and influence for women: the impending wealth transfer and the unprecedented surge in women's educational attainment. These elements are poised to catalyze a revolution in the Shero Nation, enabling women to redefine their roles in both the corporate world and society at large.

WEALTH TRANSFER

One very notable contributing factor to the evolution of the Shero Nation is the massive impending transfer of wealth. Referred to as the greatest wealth transfer in history, the aging baby boomer population is expected to pass an estimated $30 trillion of wealth to millennial children.[94]

Women are poised to inherit a sizable share from their spouses and aging parents. This transfer of wealth will put women in a unique position. We will be able to use this power of financial capital to begin changing the entire dynamic of the corporate world. As the saying goes, "Power is money, and money is power." We will be in position to use this wealth transfer to "buy" social capital! This means the flooding of opportunities to purchase, build, and buy out businesses, which will begin a massive leveling of the playing field in business. With an estimated one-third of the world's wealth under our control, we will become a sizable economic force.

Financial strength carries with it the power to initiate change. This power, historically privy to predominantly men, will change the course of corporate governance and begin the shift in social norms and organizational structuring.

EDUCATION

Another influential contributor to the shero evolution is education. As mentioned in earlier chapters, women outnumber men three to one in higher education. *The Journal of Blacks in Higher Education* consistently documents the fact that in the African American community, women hold a huge margin for degree completion over men in almost every facet of higher education.[95] They earn two-thirds of all bachelors, 70 percent of all masters, and 60 percent of all doctorates.[96] Education is catapulting the evolution forward as we continue to seek and obtain advanced degrees.

Sadly though, even as we become the most educated gender, wage disparity continues to exist. According to the 2020 Census Bureau report, earnings continue to vary greatly between men and women.[97] The median income of a man with a college degree is $74,900. On the other hand, a college-educated woman will earn just $51,600.[98] While women make up a majority of college-educated adults, that strength is not reflected in the workforce, where men continue to dominate. This may be true now, but millennial sheroes are starting and running their own businesses in record numbers. As the evolution continues, more and more companies will be owned and run by women.

With the impending wealth transfer, not only will we have the educational capital, but we will also have the financial capital! Increased educational capital gives women the upper hand in leveraging things like technology, engineering, medicine, and a host of other disciplines traditionally dominated by men. Again, no man can deny or take away our knowledge, and our journey toward equality will continue unabated and unstoppable.

BUILDING COMMUNITY AND SUPPORTING SHEROES

In the quest to empower women and elevate the Shero Nation, fostering a robust support network is essential. This section explores how a diverse range of organizations, iconic figures, and supportive allies contribute to the advancement of gender equality. From grassroots efforts to global initiatives, these elements work in concert to build a strong community that champions women and girls. We will delve into the vital roles of various support organizations dedicated to uplifting and equipping women, highlight influential female icons who inspire and drive change, and acknowledge the crucial support provided by men advocating for gender equality. Each of these facets plays a significant role in reinforcing the shero movement, ensuring its resilience and continued progress. Let us examine how these dynamic forces collectively shape and support the journey toward a more equitable world.

SUPPORT

Any form of encouragement, emotional assistance, and practical help for a specific idea or goal is considered a means of support.[99] Thousands of women's groups aim to support and uplift girls and women. I will name a few of these organizations that promote the shero evolution. These organizations are a powerful source for the grooming and cultivating of current and upcoming sheroes. Some notable female support organizations that play a huge role in the shero evolution include:

- Equality Now—founded in 1992, working to end gender-biased laws in the US and across the world
- AnitaB.org—founded in 1987, working to put women in a position to excel in the technology field
- Dress for Success—founded in 1997 with the goal of providing appropriate clothing for women to wear in interviews
- Built by Girls—encourages girls to use technology to identify and develop solutions for girls worldwide who do not have access to a traditional education
- *Muslim Girl*—formed for Muslim and non-Muslim girls to change the misconceptions surrounding Islam
- She Should Run—promoting and jumpstarting women's political careers

Sororities, community groups, and support groups form a powerful sisterhood, a necessary aspect of the shero evolution. The bonds that we have as women uplift, encourage, and support the shero movement. Together, we are a force to be reckoned with and will not be torn apart! Let no man put asunder.

FEMALE ICONS

Female icons of the past and present give us a glimpse into the world that awaits us as leaders. We have so many female icons today. The list is exhaustive, so I will limit this to the most familiar.

These female icons influence women's growth and provide us with mental and spiritual support. Michelle Obama, the late Ruth Bader Ginsburg, Maya Angelou, Oprah Winfrey, Tarana Burke, and Sheryl Sandberg are but a few of our shero sisters. Sheryl Sandberg, COO of Facebook, boldly advocates for women's advancement and supports female growth in professional industries. One of our millennial sheroes also deserves mention here: Amanda Gorman, the youngest inaugural poet in US history. She uses her platform to advocate for social justice, equality, and positive change through her powerful words and activism. They walk boldly in a power that will not allow them to back down.

Female icons keep us energized and motivated to continue to stand together. They are more than mere symbols to be admired; they are visual representations of support and inspiration for our evolution.

MALE SUPPORT

Another catalyst to our movement is male support for women's advancement. Some men, like former president Barack Obama, speak up for women's advancement. Former president Obama is big on promoting the achievement of all women in leadership positions, especially African Americans.

Then, there is the United Nations Secretary-General, António Guterres. Mr. Guterres is a big advocate for helping to push for gender equality. He calls it "unfinished business of our time."[100] They have bold vision, but they also willingly acknowledge their weaknesses and learn from their mistakes.

The power of humble narcissism is huge in the twenty-first century. The Kardashian sisters are a prime example of the power of humble narcissism. These sisters perfected the power of feminine energy and humble narcissism and used them to build an empire! Collectively, they have over 10 million female social media followers, and the numbers grow daily. They continue teaching the world that there is more than one way to skin a cat when building and harnessing female power. Kudos to these sisters!

Millennials are also perfecting the use of humble narcissism. With social media as their platform, many millennials use humble narcissism to create social media success stories as influencers and brand ambassadors. Imagine if they were acutely aware of and capitalized on the forces that are actually working for them. They would be even more fierce and formidable supporters of the shero movement!

Millennials currently embody the old saying, "Use what you got to get what you want." However, we must warn them not to misconstrue this combination as a means to an end. Recognized female energy and humble narcissism that are channeled and focused can awaken our natural creativity and resolute attitude. Millennials' importance in relation to the evolution of sheroes validates that sheroes come in all sizes, shapes, and colors, and they can wield their power using individual and collective strengths—internal, external, or otherwise.

A SHERO'S REFLECTION

With time, tenacity, and wherewithal, women have sown the seeds that birth situations where our rise in power and influence is in full motion. The impending wealth transfer, the massive advancements in higher education, community support, and all of the different ways the shero evolution is supported speak to just how preordained our evolution is. This buildup of female power and influence will ultimately shift the balance of power between the sexes. This shift will give us the capability to rewrite laws, change social perceptions, and ultimately level the playing field with the goal of coexistence with men in the realm of leadership. More importantly, it affords us the opportunity to better influence and control our own destiny, particularly when it comes to our bodies.

As women continue building businesses, running for offices, and striving to be leaders in the country and around the world, we will continue to face challenges. These challenges are sometimes blatant attacks against our gender and ability to lead and can be very difficult to endure and overcome. But we are accustomed to enduring challenges and painful situations and still thriving!

As the birthers of life, we push through excruciating pain to see a beautiful new life on the other side of that pain. Being or becoming a shero means to take in stride the challenges that society puts us through, resist discouragement to the point of giving in, and most of all let no man put asunder.

Despite sheroes moving at different speeds through varying levels and stages of their journeys, the Shero Nation has developed a momentum of its own! As more women and advocates rise in the empowering truth of creating our own wealth and capital, the evolution will continue to mature. The reference to the biblical passage "let no man put asunder" is intended to lift the spirits of those who read this book to a place of divine intervention divinity.

THE SHERO IN YOU

Not every woman immediately recognizes the shero within herself, but as she embarks on her personal journey, she uncovers her role in the collective shero movement. This transformative process requires hard work, determination, and unwavering support for fellow sheroes, but the rewards are invaluable. As we continue to evolve, it is essential to acknowledge and confront the threats and obstacles that lie ahead, approaching them with purposeful intention.

Let this book be your beacon, lighting your way and mapping out the path ahead. Face the challenges before us with unwavering courage, and embrace the limitless potential for greatness within yourself and your sisters. United and fully committed to this movement, no man can put asunder our collective strength. Together, we will gather unstoppable momentum, propelling us to our rightful place in society and the world.

I dare you, dear reader, to dive deep within and discover the shero that resides within you. May this book serve as an awakening to the realities unfolding before our eyes and ignite the fire that fuels your journey. Let us rise together, sheroes, surmounting obstacles and reaching our desired destination. The evolutionary tides are in motion, and with an indomitable force that only divine intervention can impede, we will undoubtedly reach the shores that await us!

Conclusion

As we near the end of this transformative journey, it's crucial to reflect on the comprehensive path we've traversed. This book has meticulously unveiled the societal constructs that have long constrained women's potential. Yet it's equally important to celebrate the enduring resilience of women who have transcended these limitations to become leaders and trailblazers. By internalizing the lessons learned, we can collectively foster a future where women are empowered to break free from these constraints, creating a more equitable society. This transformation is not just for today's women, but is a lasting legacy that will elevate future generations, ensuring that the foundation for gender equity remains strong, progressive, and vital.

As we move forward, it is crucial to dismantle the cultural narratives that perpetuate social stereotypes, particularly those that frame women's emotionality as a weakness. Women should be encouraged not to suppress their emotions but to embrace them as a powerful asset. Emotional intelligence—awareness, empathy, and the ability to navigate complex human dynamics—is an indispensable quality that enhances leadership today. By owning their emotional tendencies and redefining what it means to lead with emotion, women can break free from outdated molds and demonstrate that effective leadership is not about detachment but rather about connection, compassion, and resilience.

However, this change cannot rest solely on the shoulders of women. It requires a collective organizational shift to recognize and value the strength that emotional intelligence brings to leadership across all levels. We all, regardless of gender, must play a part in this shift. Companies must foster environments that allow diverse expressions of leadership, where emotional authenticity is not seen as a liability but as a vital leadership tool. By doing so, we can dismantle the barriers created by outdated perceptions, ultimately paving the way for a new generation of leaders—both women and men—who can thrive beyond the rigid confines of traditional gender norms. This inclusive approach will lead to more adaptive, compassionate, and effective leadership styles better suited for the complexities of our modern world.

As we conclude this book, it is evident that empowering women to overcome societal constraints is not just a call to action but a vital and urgent necessity. The reflections shared throughout these chapters propel us toward a transformative path, one where we collectively reframe the narrative surrounding women's leadership and emotional expression.

We must carry this legacy forward, recognizing the interplay between personal agency and cultural forces. As we strive for a more inclusive society, may we continue to find strength in our diverse experiences, advocate for change, and inspire future generations to break through the Glass Cliffs and other barriers that seek to limit their potential. Together, we must illuminate the path to empowerment, ensuring every woman can rise, thrive, and redefine what it means to lead authentically in a world filled with challenges.

By exploring the multifaceted concept of a shero, we come to understand the profound impact of standing as a beacon of strength and resilience. Sheroes, whether they are bold leaders in the public eye or silent warriors within their communities, embody the transformative power of womanhood. As we celebrate their contributions, we must remain vigilant against the threats of objectification buy-in and the pitfalls of narcissism that loom over millennial women. The insidious nature of objectification undermines our authentic identity and diminishes the strides we strive to make for gender equality. When women internalize superficial societal standards, they inadvertently contribute to a narrative that sidelines their true capabilities. Simultaneously, the misconception that millennials are a "narcissistic generation" demands critical examination. At the same time that self-focus can foster empowerment, it risks devolving into self-absorption if the purpose is not actively pursued. We must challenge these limitations, encouraging young women to recognize their inherent worth and power. By fostering a culture that values contributions over appearances and encourages authentic connection with one another, we can pave the way for a future where sheroes thrive unabated. Ultimately, as we empower the next generation, we honor our shared histories and forge a resilient path forward, ensuring that every woman can confidently embrace her identity as a shero without apology.

Today, as we stand on the shoulders of giants, the fight for true equality continues with urgency. The evolving role of women, fortified by the strength of community and shared purpose, serves as a testament to what has been achieved and what remains to be done. We are responsible for continuing this legacy, ensuring that every woman can unapologetically claim her identity as a shero, paving the way for future generations to thrive without boundaries. In acknowledging our past, we empower ourselves to forge a more equitable future firmly rooted in resilience, hope, and unwavering determination.

The journey from suppression to self-actualization is evident, as countless women have transformed their lives, defied societal expectations, and embraced their identities as leaders and pioneers. Drawing from the historical struggles of our predecessors, we recognize that the legacy of the suffrage movement and subsequent battles for equality laid the groundwork for our collective evolution.

As we navigate the challenges ahead, we are fortified by the support of our community and the impending wealth transfer. We uphold the promise that no adversary, be it internal or external, can sever the bonds that unite us. The phrase "let no man put asunder" resonates deeply within our movement, reflecting our commitment to preserving the empowerment of sheroes everywhere. It underscores our resolve to nurture the female energy and humble narcissism that propel us forward, reminding us that the Shero Nation is not just a possibility but an inevitable reality. Together, we will rise, disrupt outdated paradigms, and create a future where every woman can thrive unapologetically, ensuring that the spirit of the Shero Nation remains unyielding and ever present.

EMBRACING THE SHERO JOURNEY

As we conclude this exploration of the Shero Nation, it's imperative to reflect on the powerful themes woven throughout our journey. Each chapter has illuminated the strength found in community, the importance of reclaiming our narratives, and the unwavering spirit of women forging paths in a world often dominated by patriarchal norms. The stories shared—from the quiet resilience of a single mother fighting for her children's future to the outspoken activist challenging systemic injustice—serve as testaments to our collective power.

Consider your own life and the unyielding shero within you. Remember when you chose to speak up in meetings where your voice felt diminished, or you supported a fellow woman facing challenges in her career? These small yet significant actions contribute to the broader movement, illustrating that we do not need to act defiantly to disrupt the status quo; instead, we can navigate our roles with grace and strength, embodying empowerment without rebellion.

The mindset of self-objectification and misplaced narcissism can be redefined as we embrace our multifaceted identities. Let us shift the paradigm to celebrate authentic self-worth rooted in our capabilities, accomplishments, and connections. This journey teaches us that our value is not based on superficial measures but on our contributions to the world and those around us.

As you close this book, carry with you the priceless knowledge gained and the responsibilities that come with it. Share these insights with your friends, family, and community. Encourage conversations, spark discussions, and reach out to those who can amplify the shero message—whether through podcasts, social media platforms, or television forums. The call to action is clear: we must unite, lift each other, and spread our narrative far and wide.

Your participation in the shero movement is not just an act of support but a commitment to effecting change, fostering unity, and nurturing future generations of strong, empowered women. Together, we shall continue to rise, unyielding and ever present, forging a landscape where every woman can thrive unapologetically. Stand with us, and let's build the Shero Nation together. To fuel your journey and stay connected, visit www.sheronation.life for powerful insights, encouragement, and conversations on gender equality and the continued evolution of the Shero Nation. Now is the time. There is light at the end of the tunnel. The shero revolution is here.

About the Author

Dr. Barbara Walker-Green is a multifaceted entrepreneur, author, and financial professional with over twenty years of experience in empowering individuals and businesses. As the founder of Advanced Wealth and Retirement Planning Concepts, she has been instrumental in helping clients navigate complex financial landscapes, strengthening their financial well-being and future prosperity.

Barbara is also the visionary behind the Shero Nation movement, which she founded to inspire and empower individuals through motivational writings and leadership initiatives. Her influential book, *The Inevitable Rise of the Shero Nation*, has resonated with countless readers, championing a message of resilience and empowerment. Building on this success, *The Unstoppable Shero: A Woman's Guide to Thriving in a Resistant World*, is an offshoot that offers a more accessible and engaging exploration of these transformative themes.

Through her work with Shero Nation, Barbara continues to uplift and inspire through motivational writings that emphasize self-improvement, leadership, and the power of perseverance. A passionate advocate for financial literacy, gender equality, and community empowerment, she actively engages in outreach, mentorship, and public speaking to create opportunities for growth and success.

Dr. Walker-Green's unwavering commitment to excellence and her passion for helping others have established her as a true leader and a source of inspiration for those striving to reach their full potential.

Dr. Barbara Walker-Green

Dr. Barbara Walker-Green lives in Houston, TX and is pleased to connect with her readers professionally and socially!

Website: www.Sheronation.com
LinkedIn: https://www.linkedin.com/company/sheronation/
Facebook: https://www.facebook.com/sheronationlife
Instagram: https://www.instagram.com/sheronationlife/

For professional and media inquiries, speaking engagements, and questions about Dr. Barbara Walker-Green, you can reach her directly at www.drbarbarawalkergreen.com

SHERO NATION
WHERE YOUR PATH MEETS YOUR POTENTIAL

Endnotes

1   Founders Online, "Abigail Adams to John Adams, 31 March 1776," National Archives, https://founders.archives.gov/documents/Adams/04-01-02-0241.

2   Alice H. Eagly and Steven J. Karau, "Role Congruity Theory of Prejudice toward Female Leaders," *Psychological Review* 109, no. 3 (2002): 573–98, https://doi.org/10.1037/0033-295x.109.3.573.

3   Eagly and Karau, 573.

4   Eagly and Karau.

5   Eagly and Karau, 568–70.

6   Andrea Fischbach, Philipp W. Lichtenthaler, and Nina Horstmann, "Leadership and Gender Stereotyping of Emotions," *Journal of Personnel Psychology* 14, no. 3 (2015): 153–62, https://doi.org/10.1027/1866-5888/a000136.

7   Fischbach et al., 152.

8   Virginia E. Schein, "Sex Role Stereotyping, Ability and Performance: Prior Research and New Directions," *Personnel Psychology* 31, no. 2 (1978): 259–68, https://doi.org/10.1111/j.1744-6570.1978.tb00445.x.

9   Meghna Sabharwal, "From Glass Ceiling to Glass Cliff: Women in Senior Executive Service," *Journal of Public Administration Research and Theory* 25, no. 2 (2013): 399–426, https://doi.org/10.1093/jopart/mut030.

10   Terrance W. Fitzsimmons and Victor J. Callan, "Applying a Capital Per-
      spective to Explain Continued Gender Inequality in the C-Suite," *The
      Leadership Quarterly* 27, no. 3 (2016): 354–70, https://doi.org/10.1016/j.
      leaqua.2015.11.003.

11   Fitzsimmons and Callan, 358.

12   Fitzsimmons and Callan, 360.

13   Sabharwal.

14   Victoria L. Brescoll, "Leading with Their Hearts? How Gender Stereo-
      types of Emotion Lead to Biased Evaluations of Female Leaders," *The
      Leadership Quarterly* 27, no. 3 (2016): 415–28, https://doi.org/10.1016/j.
      leaqua.2016.02.005.

15   Brescoll, 427.

16   Brescoll, 418.

17   Brescoll, 416.

18   McKinsey & Company and LeanIn.org, "Women in the Workplace 2019,"
      2019, https://womenintheworkplace.com/.

19   Fitzsimmons and Callan.

20   Fitzsimmons and Callan; Avigail Moor, Ayala Cohen, and Ortal Beeri, "In
      Quest of Excellence, Not Power: Women's Paths to Positions of Influence
      and Leadership," *Advancing Women in Leadership* 35, no. 1 (2014): 1–11,
      https://search.proquest.com/openview/932389c9e1615aa6b940938ecabaae
      f9/1?pq-origsite=gscholar&cbl=44345.

21   A. Moor, A. Cohen, and O. Beeri, "In Quest of Excellence, Not Power:
      Women's Paths to Positions of Influence and Leadership," *Advancing Women
      in Leadership* 35, no. 1 (2014): 1–11, https://search.proquest.com/openview
      /932389c9e1615aa6b940938ecabaaef9/1?pq-origsite=gscholar&cbl=44345.

22 Judith G. Oakley, "Gender-Based Barriers to Senior Management Positions: Understanding the Scarcity of Female CEOs," *Journal of Business Ethics* 27, no. 4 (2000): 321–34, https://doi.org/10.1023/a:1006226129868.

23 Fitzsimmons and Callan, 355.

24 Fitzsimmons and Callan, 357.

25 Barbara White, Charles Cox, and Cary L. Cooper, *Women's Career Development: A Study of High Flyers* (Oxford: Blackwell Publishing, 1992).

26 Laura Doey, Robert J. Coplan, and Mila Kingsbury, "Bashful Boys and Coy Girls: A Review of Gender Differences in Childhood Shyness," *Sex Roles* 70, no. 7–8 (2013): 255–66, https://doi.org/10.1007/s11199-013-0317-9.

27 Fitzsimmons and Callan, 359.

28 Craig E. Johnson, *Meeting the Ethical Challenges of Leadership: Casting Light or Shadow* (London: Sage, 2011).

29 Fitzsimmons and Callan, 355.

30 Fitzsimmons and Callan, 356.

31 Fitzsimmons and Callan, 357.

32 Irving L. Janis, "Groupthink," *Psychology Today* 26 (1971): 43–76.

33 Oakley, 325.

34 Brescoll, 41.

35 Fitzsimmons and Callan.

36 Brescoll; Eagly and Karau; Fitzsimmons and Callan; Oakley; Schein.

37 Oakley, 329.

38 McKinsey & Company and LeanIn.org.

39   Ivan P. Pavlov, *The Work of the Digestive Glands* (London: Griffin, 1897/1902).

40   D. A. Van Hemert, F. J. R. Van de Vijver, and A. J. J. M. Vingerhoets, "Culture and Crying: Prevalences and Gender Differences," *Cross-Cultural Research* 45, no. 4 (2011): 399–431, https://doi.org/10.1177/1069397111404519.

41   J. Archer, "Testosterone and Human Aggression: An Evaluation of the Challenge Hypothesis," Neuroscience & Biobehavioral Reviews 30, no. 3 (2006): 319–45, https://doi.org/10.1016/j.neubiorev.2004.12.007; O. C. Schultheiss and A. Schiepe-Tiska, "Hormonal Basis of Human Aggression: Insights from Studies Using the Implicit Association Test," In *International Handbook of Anger: Constituent and Concomitant Biological, Psychological, and Social Processes*, ed. M. Potegal, G. Stemmler, and C. Spielberger (Springer 2013), 55–71, https://doi.org/10.1007/978-0-387-89676-2_4.

42   S. E. Taylor and G. C. Gonzaga, "Nurturing and Bonding: The Role of Oxytocin and Progesterone," *Hormones and Behavior* 50, no. 4 (2006): 605–10, https://doi.org/10.1016/j.yhbeh.2006.06.028.

43   American Psychological Association, *Stress in America: The State of Our Nation*, 2017, https://www.apa.org/news/press/releases/stress/2017/state-nation.pdf.

44   J. Smith, "The Influence of Gender on Emotional Expression in Leadership," *Journal of Leadership Studies* 14, no. 3 (2020): 45–62, https://doi.org/10.1002/jls.21345.

45   L. Taylor, "Revisiting Gender Stereotypes: A Study on Emotional Expression across Cultures," *Journal of Cross-Cultural Psychology* 52, no. 7 (2021): 876–93, https://doi.org/10.1177/00220221211009845.

46   Harvard Business School, "The Dynamics of Gender and Leadership: Insights on Emotional Intelligence and Empathy," 2022, https://www.hbs.edu/faculty/Pages/item.aspx?num=57020.

47   Natalie Wolchover, "Men vs. Women: Our Key Physical Differences Explained," LiveScience, September 22, 2011, https://www.livescience.com/33513-men-vs-women-our-physical-differences-explained.html.

48   See the following sources: P. Skerrett, "Men's vs. Women's Bodies: How Our Anatomies Differ," Harvard Health Publishing, 2016, https://www.health.harvard.edu/blog/mens-vs-womens-bodies-how-our-anatomies-differ-2016070810044; D. A. Puts, "Beauty and the Beast: Mechanisms of Sexual Selection in Humans," *Evolution and Human Behavior* 31, no. 3 (2010): 157–75, https://doi.org/10.1016/j.evolhumbehav.2010.02.005; M. M. Grumbach and R. J. Auchus, "Estrogen: Consequences for Women and Men," *The Journal of Clinical Endocrinology & Metabolism* 84, no. 5 (1999): 1392–9, https://doi.org/10.1210/jcem.84.5.5660; C. J. Ley, B. Lees, and J. C. Stevenson, "Sex- and Menopause-Associated Changes in Body-Fat Distribution," *The American Journal of Clinical Nutrition* 55, no. 5 (1992): 950–4, https://doi.org/10.1093/ajcn/55.5.950; W. D. Lassek and S. J. C. Gaulin, "Changes in Body Fat Distribution in Relation to Parity in American Women: A Covert Form of Maternal Depletion," *American Journal of Physical Anthropology* 131, no. 2 (2006): 295–302, https://doi.org/10.1002/ajpa.20393.

49   Fitzsimmons and Callan, 357.

50   Bureau of Labor Statistics, "Labor Force Statistics from the Current Population Survey: Employed Persons by Detailed Occupation, Sex, Race, and Hispanic or Latino Ethnicity," US Department of Labor, 2024, https://www.bls.gov/cps/cpsaat11.htm; CFP Board, "Racial Diversity in the Financial Planning Profession," Certified Financial Planner Board of Standards, 2024, https://www.cfp.net/knowledge/reports-and-statistics/racial-diversity-in-financial-planning.

51   Merriam-Webster Dictionary, "Glass ceiling," https://www.merriam-webster.com/dictionary/glass%20ceiling.

52   G. Back, "The Glass Cliff Phenomenon: Why Women Are More Likely to Be Appointed to Leadership Positions during Times of Crisis," *Marie Claire*, 2020, https://www.marieclaire.com.au/glass-cliff-theory.

53   K. Caprino, "The 'Glass Cliff' Phenomenon That Senior Female Leaders Face Today," *Forbes*, 2018, https://www.forbes.com/sites/kathycaprino/2018/01/21/the-glass-cliff-phenomenon-that-senior-female-leaders-face-today.

54   Yael S. Oelbaum, "Understanding the Glass Cliff Effect: Why Are Female Leaders Being Pushed toward the Edge?" CUNY Academic Works, 2016, https://academicworks.cuny.edu/gc_etds/1597.

55 Susanna Whawell, "Women in Boardrooms Falling Off 'Glass Cliff,' Research Shows," *Independent,* April 30, 2018, https://www.independent.co.uk/news/long_reads/glass-cliff-female-leaders-women-boardrooms-research-gender-pay-gap-reporting-a8312666.html.

56 Michelle K. Ryan, S. Alexander Haslam, and Tom Postmes, "Reactions to the Glass Cliff: Gender Differences in Explanations for the Precariousness of Women's Leadership Positions," *Journal of Organizational Change Management* 20, no. 2 (2007): 182–97, https://doi.org/10.1108/09534810710724748.

57 Caprino 2018.

58 Caprino 2018.

59 Aaron Gregg, "General Dynamics CEO Phebe Novakovic Recounts Her National Security Journey, Takes a Jab at Silicon Valley," *The Washington Post,* June 28, 2019, https://www.washingtonpost.com/business/2019/06/28/general-dynamics-ceo-phebe-novakovic-recounts-her-national-security-journey-takes-jab-silicon-valley/.

60 Hewlett Packard, "HP Names Meg Whitman President and Chief Executive Officer," news release, September 22, 2011, https://www.sec.gov/Archives/edgar/data/47217/000110465911052939/a11-26875_1ex99d1.htm.

61 Catherine J. Taylor, "Occupational Sex Composition and the Gendered Availability of Workplace Support," *Gender & Society* 24, no. 2 (2010): 189–212, https://doi.org/10.1177/0891243209359912.

62 Oakley, 329.

63 Alison Cook and Christy Glass, "Above the Glass Ceiling: When Are Women and Racial/Ethnic Minorities Promoted to CEO?" *Strategic Management Journal* 35, no. 7 (2013): 1080–89, https://doi.org/10.1002/smj.2161.

64 M. K. Ryan and S. A. Haslam, "The Glass Cliff: Evidence that Women Are Overrepresented in Precarious Leadership Positions," *British Journal of Management* 16, no. 2 (2005): 81–90.

65   S. Whawell, "Why women in senior positions choose to step away: An investigation into the career motivations, experiences and decision-making of senior female legal professionals in England and Wales," PhD, Diss., Alliance Manchester Business School, 2023

66   Caprino 2018.

67   Yael S. Oelbaum "Understanding the Glass Cliff Effect: Why Are Female Leaders Being Pushed Toward the Edge?" PhD, Diss., City University of New York, 2016.

68   Ryan and Haslam 2005.

69   Whawell 2023.

70   Merriam-Webster Dictionary, "Shero," https://www.merriam-webster.com/dictionary/shero.

71   The Urban Dictionary, "Shero," https://www.urbandictionary.com/define.php?term=shero.

72   Fitzsimmons and Callan.

73   Fitzsimmons and Callan, 355.

74   Fitzsimmons and Callan, 356.

75   Allen St. John, "Is Richard Williams, Serena and Venus's Dad, the Greatest Coach of All Time?" *Forbes*, January 28, 2017, https://www.forbes.com/sites/allenstjohn/2017/01/28/is-richard-williams-serena-and-venuss-dad-the-greatest-coach-of-all-time/.

76   Kristen Bialik and Richard Fry, "How Millennials Compare with Prior Generations," Pew Research Center's Social and Demographic Trends Project, February 14, 2019, https://www.pewsocialtrends.org/essay/millennial-life-how-young-adulthood-today-compares-with-prior-generations/.

77   Mayo Clinic, "Narcissistic Personality Disorder," Mayo Foundation for Medical Education and Research, November 18, 2017, https://www.mayoclinic.

org/diseases-conditions/narcissistic-personality-disorder/symptoms-causes/
syc-20366662.

78   Kira M. Newman, "The Surprisingly Boring Truth about Millennials and Narcissism," *Greater Good*, The Greater Good Science Center at the University
of California, Berkeley, January 17, 2018, https://greatergood.berkeley.edu/
article/item/the_surprisingly_boring_truth_about_millennials_and_narcissism.

79   Michael Maccoby, "Narcissistic Leaders: The Incredible Pros, the Inevitable
Cons," *Harvard Business Review*, February 1, 2000, https://hbr.org/2004/01/
narcissistic-leaders-the-incredible-pros-the-inevitable-cons.

80   Maccoby.

81   Julia Brailovskaia and Hans-Werner Bierhoff, "The Narcissistic Millennial Generation: A Study of Personality Traits and Online Behavior on
Facebook," *Journal of Adult Development* 27, no. 1 (2018): 23–35, https://doi.
org/10.1007/s10804-018-9321-1; Niraj Chokshi, "Attention Young People:
This Narcissism Study Is All About You," *New York Times*, May 15, 2019,
https://www.nytimes.com/2019/05/15/science/narcissism-teenagers.html.

82   Lesley Rennis, Gloria McNamara, Erica Seidel, and Yuliya Shneyderman,
"Google It!: Urban Community College Students' Use of the Internet to
Obtain Self-Care and Personal Health Information," *College Student Journal*
49, no. 3 (2015): 414–26.

83   Walker-Green 2019.

84   National Park Service, "19th Amendment," accessed October 1, 2024, https://
www.nps.gov/subjects/womenshistory/19th-amendment.htm.

85   Hunt.

86   Andrew Schneider, "Meet 'Black Girl Magic,' the 19 African-American
Women Elected as Judges in Texas," NPR, January 16, 2019, https://www.
npr.org/2019/01/16/685815783/meet-black-girl-magic-the-19-african-
American-women-elected-as-judges-in-Texas.

87   Eagly and Karau, 590.

88   Eagly and Karau, 591.

89   Tomas Chamorro-Premuzic and Avivah Wittenberg-Cox, "Will the Pandemic Reshape Notions of Female Leadership?" *Harvard Business Review*, June 26, 2020, https://hbr.org/2020/06/will-the-pandemic-reshape-notions-of-female-leadership.

90   Rob Dube, "Compassionate Leadership Can Create a Better Economy and a Happier World," *Forbes*, August 3, 2020, https://www.forbes.com/sites/robdube/2020/08/03/compassionate-leadership-can-create-a-better-economy-and-a-happier-world/.

91   Bethany Garner, "Female Leadership during COVID-19: What Can We Learn?" Business Because, June 19, 2020, https://www.businessbecause.com/news/insights/7028/learn-female-leadership-covid-19.

92   Shelley Zalis, "In the COVID-19 Era, Female Leaders Are Shining—Here's Why," MSNBC, June 9, 2020, https://www.msnbc.com/know-your-value/covid-19-era-female-leaders-are-shining-here-s-why-n1227931.

93   Abraham. H. Maslow, "A Theory of Human Motivation," *Psychological Review* 50 (1943): 370–96.

94   Mark Hall, "The Greatest Wealth Transfer in History: What's Happening and What Are the Implications?" *Forbes*, November 12, 2019, https://www.forbes.com/sites/markhall/2019/11/11/the-greatest-wealth-transfer-in-history-whats-happening-and-what-are-the-implications/.

95   "African Americans Show a Major Increase in Higher Education Degrees at All Levels, but Black Women Continue to Far Outpace Black Men," *The Journal of Blacks in Higher Education* no. 49 (2005): 28, https://doi.org/10.2307/25073292; "Black Women Far Outdistance Black Men in Doctoral Degree Awards: But How Are They Doing Compared to White Women?" *The Journal of Blacks in Higher Education* no. 26 (1999): 69, https://doi.org/10.2307/2999163.

96   National Center for Education Statistics, "Degrees Conferred by Race and Sex," US Department of Education, accessed August 12, 2020, https://nces.ed.gov/fastfacts/display.asp?id=72.

97   United States Census Bureau, "Income and Poverty in the United States: 2018," June 26, 2020, https://www.census.gov/library/publications/2019/demo/p60-266.html.

98   Richard Fry, "U.S. Women Near Milestone in the College-Educated Labor Force," Pew Research Center, August 7, 2020, https://www.pewresearch.org/fact-tank/2019/06/20/u-s-women-near-milestone-in-the-college-educated-labor-force/.

99   Cambridge Dictionary: English Dictionary, Translations and Thesaurus, "Support," accessed August 12, 2020, https://dictionary.cambridge.org/.

www.ingramcontent.com/pod-product-compliance
Lightning Source LLC
Chambersburg PA
CBHW031536260326
41914CB00032B/1832/J